AI-Powered Project Management

Merging Technology with Team Success

By Mohammad Zaripour

Copyright © 2024 by Mohammad Zaripour

Title: AI-Powered Project Management: Merging Technology with Team Success

Author: Mohammad Zaripour

All rights reserved. No part of this book may be reproduced, stored in a retrieval system, or transmitted in any form or by any means, electronic, mechanical, photocopying, recording, or otherwise, without the prior written permission of the publisher, except for brief quotations used in reviews or scholarly works.

Thanks

Mohammad Zaripour

About the Author

Mohammad Zaripour is a distinguished professional with extensive expertise in project management and engineering, specializing in the integration of artificial intelligence (AI) to enhance project outcomes. With a robust foundation in both traditional and agile project management practices, Mohammad has cultivated a deep understanding of how AI can transform project management processes and drive team success.

Certifications and Qualifications

Project Management Professional (PMP): Awarded by the Project Management Institute (PMI), the PMP certification reflects Mohammad's advanced skills and knowledge in leading and directing projects. This credential underscores his ability to manage the complete project lifecycle, from planning and execution to monitoring and closing, with a focus on delivering successful outcomes.

PMI Agile Certified Practitioner (PMI-ACP): This certification recognizes Mohammad's proficiency in agile methodologies, including Scrum, Kanban, and Lean. It highlights his capability to adapt to changing project environments and effectively manage projects using agile principles, ensuring flexibility and high-quality results.

Professional Scrum Master (PSM): Offered by Scrum.org, the PSM certification validates Mohammad's expertise in Scrum, an agile framework for managing complex projects. This credential demonstrates his ability to facilitate Scrum teams, uphold Scrum practices, and drive continuous improvement within project teams.

Engineer-in-Training (EIT): This certification represents Mohammad's strong foundation in engineering principles and his commitment to professional development. As a step towards becoming a licensed Professional Engineer (PE), the EIT certification showcases his technical proficiency and dedication to excellence in engineering.

Professional Background

Mohammad's career is marked by his successful application of project management and engineering skills across diverse industries. His unique ability to integrate technical knowledge with project management expertise has been instrumental in achieving project goals and driving innovation. Mohammad's approach is defined by strategic planning, effective communication, and a commitment to leveraging AI technologies to optimize project performance.

Personal Philosophy

Mohammad is passionate about continuous learning and the transformative potential of AI in project management. His certifications reflect his dedication to staying current with industry best practices and methodologies. He is committed to sharing his knowledge and helping others excel in managing complex projects through the innovative application of AI.

In *AI-Powered Project Management: Merging Technology with Team Success*, Mohammad draws on his extensive qualifications and experience to provide practical insights and actionable advice. His expertise in both traditional and agile project management, combined with his solid engineering background, equips him to offer valuable perspectives on harnessing AI to enhance project management practices and achieve greater team success.

Table of content

Introduction: 11
Chapter 1 16
Chapter 2 22
Chapter 3 29
Chapter 4 37
Chapter 5 45
Chapter 6 52
Chapter 7 60
Chapter 8 68
Chapter 9 77
Chapter 10 86
Chapter 11 95
Chapter 12 103
Chapter 13 112
Chapter 14 120
Chapter 15 128
Chapter 16 136
Conclusion 143
Appendices 148
References 154
Glossary 161

Abstract:

In an era where technology continuously reshapes the way we work, project management is undergoing a revolutionary transformation. "AI-Powered Project Management: Merging Technology with Team Success" delves into the dynamic intersection of artificial intelligence and project management, offering a comprehensive guide for leaders and teams navigating this new landscape.

This book explores how AI is no longer just a futuristic concept but an integral part of modern project management practices. It provides readers with a deep understanding of how AI tools can enhance decision-making, optimize workflows, and drive efficiency across all stages of a project. From task automation and predictive analytics to intelligent resource allocation and real-time data insights, AI is redefining the role of the project manager, enabling them to focus on strategy, creativity, and team collaboration.

However, technology alone cannot guarantee success. This book emphasizes the importance of merging AI with the human element—fostering a culture of adaptability, continuous learning, and effective communication. It highlights how AI can empower teams to achieve greater synergy, reduce risks, and deliver projects that meet or exceed expectations.

"AI-Powered Project Management: Merging Technology with Team Success" also addresses the challenges and ethical considerations of implementing AI in project management. It provides practical strategies for overcoming resistance to change, ensuring data privacy, and maintaining transparency in decision-making processes.

Through case studies, real-world examples, and actionable insights, this book equips project managers, team leaders, and business executives with the knowledge and tools they need to leverage AI effectively. Whether you are leading a small team or managing large-scale projects, this book offers valuable guidance on how to integrate AI into your project management practices, ultimately driving innovation, enhancing productivity, and achieving sustainable success.

Introduction:

Introduction:

Welcome to "AI-Powered Project Management: Merging Technology with Team Success." If you've picked up this book, you're likely curious about how artificial intelligence (AI) can change the way we manage projects. Perhaps you've heard about AI in the news or seen it slowly creeping into your workplace, and now you're wondering how it fits into the world of project management. Well, you've come to the right place.

In recent years, AI has moved from the realm of science fiction into our everyday lives. It's in the phones we carry, the cars we drive, and even the smart devices that help us manage our homes. But its potential doesn't stop there. AI is now making its way into the workplace, and it's set to transform how we manage projects, collaborate with teams, and achieve our goals.

But what does this mean for project managers? For some, the idea of AI might seem daunting, like something out of a sci-fi movie where machines take over. But the reality is far more practical and exciting. AI in project management isn't about replacing people; it's about enhancing the way we work. Imagine having tools that can predict project risks before they happen, automate repetitive tasks, and provide insights that help you make better decisions. That's the power of AI.

This book is your guide to understanding how AI can be a valuable ally in your project management toolkit. We'll explore what AI is, how it works, and most importantly, how it can be applied to make your projects more successful. Whether you're managing a small team on a tight deadline or overseeing a large, complex project, AI has something to offer. It can help you streamline processes, improve accuracy, and free up your time to focus on what really matters—leading your team and delivering great results.

But it's not just about the technology. This book also emphasizes the importance of the human element in project management. After all, even the most advanced AI tools need skilled project managers and engaged teams to make them work. We'll look at how to integrate AI into your projects in a way that enhances, rather than replaces, the strengths that people bring to the table. We'll also discuss the challenges you might face, from ethical considerations to the fear of change, and how to navigate them successfully.

By the end of this book, you'll have a clear understanding of how AI can transform your approach to project management. You'll be equipped with practical strategies and insights that you can apply right away, whether you're new to AI or already exploring its possibilities. Together, we'll discover how AI and human intelligence can work hand in hand to achieve greater success in any project.

So, let's dive in and explore the exciting world of AI-powered project management. Your journey into the future of work starts here.

Part 1

Foundations of AI in Project Management

Chapter 1

Chapter 1

What is Artificial Intelligence?

Artificial Intelligence, or AI, is a term that's been buzzing around in conversations, news articles, and even in everyday life. But what exactly is AI, and why is it becoming such a significant part of how we live and work? In this chapter, we'll explore what AI truly means, breaking down the concept into understandable terms, and examining its relevance in today's world, particularly in the realm of project management.

At its core, AI refers to the ability of machines to perform tasks that would typically require human intelligence. These tasks can range from simple activities, like recognizing patterns in data, to more complex functions, like making decisions based on past experiences or even learning from new information. The idea is to create systems that can think, learn, and adapt—much like a human would—allowing them to solve problems, understand language, and even perceive their environment.

To understand AI, it's important to grasp the basics of how it works. AI is powered by algorithms, which are essentially sets of rules or instructions that a machine follows to complete a task. These algorithms can be simple or complex, depending on what the AI is designed to do. For example, a basic AI might be programmed to recognize patterns in numbers, while a more advanced AI could be capable of analyzing large sets of data to predict future trends.

There are different types of AI, each with varying levels of complexity and capability. Narrow AI, also known as weak AI, is designed to perform a specific task. This is the most common form of AI we encounter today. It powers everything from your smartphone's voice assistant to the algorithms that recommend movies on your favorite streaming service. Narrow AI is excellent at performing the tasks it's designed for, but it doesn't possess general intelligence or understanding beyond those tasks.

On the other hand, General AI, or strong AI, is a more advanced concept—one that remains largely theoretical at this stage. General AI would have the ability to understand, learn, and apply knowledge across a wide range of tasks, much like a human being. While we aren't there yet, the pursuit of General AI is a significant area of research, with potential implications that could reshape many aspects of our lives.

A crucial element of AI's functionality is machine learning. Machine learning allows AI systems to improve over time by learning from data. Instead of being explicitly programmed for every task, a machine learning model can analyze data, recognize patterns, and make decisions or predictions based on that information. For example, an AI that monitors project timelines might learn to predict delays based on past project data, adjusting future timelines to improve accuracy.

Deep learning, a subset of machine learning, goes a step further by using neural networks to process data in ways that mimic the human brain. These neural networks enable AI to recognize complex patterns, such as identifying objects in images or understanding natural language. This is the technology behind many advanced AI applications, from self-driving cars to sophisticated language translation services.

The journey of AI from concept to reality has been long and fascinating. The idea of creating intelligent machines dates back to ancient civilizations, where myths and stories often depicted artificial beings endowed with intelligence. However, the modern field of AI began in the mid-20th century, with pioneers like Alan Turing and John McCarthy laying the groundwork for what would become one of the most exciting fields of technological development.

AI's evolution has been marked by breakthroughs and challenges. Early AI research in the 1950s and 1960s focused on creating algorithms that could solve logical problems or play games like chess. These early systems were impressive for their time but limited by the technology available. It wasn't until the advent of more powerful computers and the vast amounts of data generated in the digital age that AI began to make significant strides.

Today, AI is a reality in many aspects of our lives. It powers the apps we use, influences the decisions we make, and is increasingly finding its way into the workplace. In project management, AI offers the potential to transform how we plan, execute, and evaluate projects. By automating routine tasks, providing insights through data analysis, and even predicting project outcomes, AI is set to become an indispensable tool for project managers.

However, understanding AI is not just about knowing how it works. It's also about appreciating the opportunities and challenges it presents. AI can enhance productivity, but it also raises questions about the future of work, the ethical use of technology, and the balance between human and machine intelligence. As we move forward, project managers will need to navigate these questions, ensuring that AI is used in ways that benefit both their teams and their projects.

In this chapter, we've laid the foundation for understanding AI—what it is, how it works, and why it matters. As we move into the following chapters, we'll explore how AI can be applied specifically in project management, transforming the way we approach our work and setting the stage for greater success in our projects.

Chapter 2

Chapter 2

The Role of AI in Project Management

As technology continues to advance, project management is evolving in ways that were once unimaginable. The introduction of artificial intelligence (AI) into this field is a game-changer, promising to revolutionize how projects are planned, executed, and completed. In this chapter, we'll dive into the role of AI in project management, exploring how it's transforming traditional methods and offering new possibilities for success.

Traditionally, project management has been a complex juggling act involving the coordination of resources, timelines, budgets, and people. Project managers have had to rely on their experience, intuition, and a variety of tools to keep everything on track. While these methods have served us well, they are not without their challenges. Human error, unforeseen risks, and the ever-changing dynamics of teams can all contribute to project delays and failures.

This is where AI steps in. By leveraging AI technologies, project managers can now enhance every aspect of their work, from planning to execution. AI brings a level of precision and efficiency that was previously out of reach. It's not about replacing the project manager but about providing them with the tools to work smarter, not harder.

One of the most significant contributions of AI to project management is its ability to analyze vast amounts of data quickly and accurately. In the past, project managers might have spent hours or even days sifting through data to identify trends, assess risks, or make decisions. AI can perform these tasks in a fraction of the time, offering insights that would be difficult, if not impossible, to obtain manually.

For instance, AI-powered analytics can help project managers forecast potential risks before they become problems. By analyzing historical project data, AI can identify patterns that might indicate future issues, such as budget overruns, timeline delays, or resource shortages. This predictive capability allows project managers to take proactive measures, adjusting plans and resources to mitigate risks before they escalate.

In addition to risk management, AI plays a crucial role in optimizing project schedules. Traditional scheduling often involves complex calculations and adjustments as project variables change. AI can automate much of this process, dynamically adjusting schedules based on real-time data. If a delay occurs in one area, AI can automatically reallocate resources or adjust timelines to minimize the impact on the overall project. This level of responsiveness helps ensure that projects stay on track, even when unexpected challenges arise.

AI also enhances the way resources are managed. Effective resource management is critical to project success, and AI can make this task significantly easier. By analyzing data on team members' skills, availability, and past performance, AI can suggest the most efficient allocation of resources for each task. This ensures that the right people are working on the right tasks at the right time, maximizing productivity and minimizing waste.

But the benefits of AI don't stop at planning and resource management. AI can also improve communication and collaboration within project teams. In today's globalized world, teams are often spread across different locations and time zones, making communication a challenge. AI-powered tools can facilitate seamless communication by providing real-time language translation, summarizing meeting notes, and even predicting communication bottlenecks before they occur. These tools help keep everyone on the same page, regardless of location or language barriers.

Furthermore, AI can assist in decision-making processes. In project management, decision-making is a constant requirement, and making the right decisions at the right time is crucial for success. AI can support project managers by providing data-driven insights and recommendations, helping them weigh the pros and cons of different options. For example, if a project is running behind schedule, AI can analyze various scenarios to determine the best course of action, such as reallocating resources, adjusting timelines, or even renegotiating deadlines with stakeholders.

It's also important to recognize the role of AI in automating routine tasks. Project management involves numerous administrative tasks, such as updating progress reports, tracking time, and managing budgets. These tasks, while necessary, can be time-consuming and take focus away from more strategic activities. AI can automate many of these tasks, freeing up the project manager to focus on higher-level responsibilities, such as guiding the team, addressing challenges, and ensuring the project aligns with broader business goals.

However, as we embrace the benefits of AI in project management, it's essential to approach its integration thoughtfully. AI is a powerful tool, but it is only as effective as the data and algorithms that drive it. Project managers need to ensure that the data used by AI systems is accurate, up-to-date, and relevant. They must also be aware of the limitations of AI and understand that while AI can provide valuable insights and recommendations, the final decision-making responsibility still rests with human managers.

Moreover, the introduction of AI into project management requires a shift in mindset. Teams may need to adapt to new ways of working, and project managers must be prepared to lead this change. This includes providing training, fostering a culture of continuous learning, and ensuring that AI tools are used in a way that enhances, rather than disrupts, team dynamics.

In this chapter, we've explored the transformative role of AI in project management. By improving data analysis, risk management, scheduling, resource allocation, communication, and decision-making, AI is helping project managers deliver projects more efficiently and effectively. As we move forward, it's clear that AI will become an increasingly integral part of project management, offering new opportunities to achieve success in a fast-paced, ever-changing world.

Chapter 3

Chapter 3

AI-Driven Project Management Processes

The integration of artificial intelligence (AI) into project management is not just about using smart tools; it's about fundamentally transforming how projects are managed from start to finish. AI has the potential to reshape every step of the project management process, making it more efficient, accurate, and responsive to change. In this chapter, we'll delve into how AI-driven processes are revolutionizing project management, helping teams achieve better results with less effort.

At the heart of any successful project is a well-structured plan. Traditionally, project planning has been a labor-intensive process, requiring project managers to map out every detail, anticipate potential risks, and allocate resources carefully. While these tasks are crucial, they can be prone to errors and oversights, especially in complex projects with many moving parts. This is where AI can make a significant difference.

AI-driven project management processes begin with enhanced planning and scheduling. AI can analyze historical data from previous projects, identifying patterns and trends that can inform the planning of new projects. For example, if past projects in a similar domain encountered delays due to resource shortages, AI can highlight this as a potential risk in the planning phase, prompting the project manager to allocate resources more conservatively or build in contingency plans.

Once the project is underway, AI continues to play a critical role in managing schedules. One of the most challenging aspects of project management is keeping the project on track when unexpected changes occur. Whether it's a sudden change in scope, an unforeseen technical issue, or a delay in delivery from a supplier, these disruptions can throw the entire project timeline into disarray. AI can help manage these changes dynamically, adjusting schedules in real-time based on the latest data.

For example, if a task is delayed, AI can automatically recalibrate the project timeline, reallocating resources or adjusting dependent tasks to minimize the impact of the delay. This ability to adapt quickly and efficiently is one of the key advantages of AI in project management. It allows teams to respond to changes without losing momentum, reducing the likelihood of cascading delays that can jeopardize the entire project.

Resource management is another area where AI-driven processes shine. Traditionally, managing resources—whether it's people, materials, or equipment—requires careful planning and constant monitoring. Over- or under-utilization of resources can lead to inefficiencies, increased costs, and missed deadlines. AI can optimize resource management by analyzing data on resource availability, skills, and workload, ensuring that each resource is used effectively.

For instance, AI can suggest the best team members for specific tasks based on their skills, past performance, and current workload. It can also identify when a particular resource is being overextended or underutilized, allowing the project manager to make adjustments before issues arise. This proactive approach to resource management helps ensure that the right resources are in the right place at the right time, contributing to smoother project execution.

Risk management is another critical component of the project management process, and AI has a unique ability to enhance this area as well. Traditional risk management often relies on the project manager's experience and intuition, supplemented by checklists and risk assessment tools. While these methods can be effective, they are inherently limited by the human capacity to process and analyze large amounts of information.

AI, on the other hand, can sift through vast amounts of data, identifying potential risks that might not be immediately apparent. For example, AI can analyze market trends, supplier performance data, and even social media sentiment to predict risks that could impact the project. This might include anticipating supply chain disruptions, predicting cost fluctuations, or identifying potential legal or regulatory challenges. By providing early warnings, AI allows project managers to take preemptive action, mitigating risks before they can affect the project's outcomes.

Moreover, AI-driven processes extend to monitoring and reporting, offering project managers real-time insights into project progress. Traditional reporting often involves manually compiling data from various sources, which can be time-consuming and prone to errors. AI automates this process, gathering data from multiple systems and generating reports that provide an accurate, up-to-date picture of the project's status.

These AI-generated reports can highlight key performance indicators (KPIs), flagging areas where the project is ahead or behind schedule, where costs are exceeding expectations, or where risks are increasing. By delivering these insights in real-time, AI enables project managers to make informed decisions quickly, keeping the project on track and within budget.

In addition to enhancing existing processes, AI can introduce entirely new capabilities to project management. For example, AI-powered predictive analytics can forecast project outcomes with remarkable accuracy. By analyzing data from past projects and current trends, AI can predict whether a project is likely to meet its goals, identify potential bottlenecks, and even suggest strategies for improvement. This predictive capability allows project managers to be more proactive, addressing issues before they escalate and making adjustments to improve the likelihood of success.

AI can also facilitate better decision-making by providing project managers with data-driven insights. In complex projects, decision-making often involves weighing multiple factors, such as cost, time, quality, and risk. AI can analyze these factors, presenting the project manager with options that are optimized for the best possible outcome. This not only saves time but also reduces the cognitive load on the project manager, allowing them to focus on strategic decisions rather than getting bogged down in the details.

However, as powerful as AI-driven processes are, they are not without their challenges. Implementing AI in project management requires careful planning and a clear understanding of the technology's capabilities and limitations. Project managers must ensure that AI tools are properly integrated into existing workflows and that team members are trained to use them effectively. Moreover, the success of AI-driven processes depends on the quality of the data they rely on; inaccurate or incomplete data can lead to flawed insights and recommendations.

In this chapter, we've explored how AI-driven processes are transforming project management. From planning and scheduling to resource management, risk management, and reporting, AI offers the potential to make project management more efficient, accurate, and responsive. By embracing these AI-driven processes, project managers can unlock new levels of productivity and success, positioning their teams to thrive in an increasingly complex and dynamic business environment.

Chapter 4

Chapter 4

AI in Resource Management

Effective resource management is the backbone of any successful project. Whether it's people, equipment, time, or money, the resources available to a project must be allocated, monitored, and managed with precision. In traditional project management, this is often a time-consuming and challenging task, requiring careful planning and constant adjustment. With the advent of artificial intelligence (AI), resource management has undergone a transformation, offering new ways to optimize the use of resources and enhance project outcomes. In this chapter, we will explore how AI is redefining resource management in project management, making it more efficient, adaptive, and intelligent.

At the core of resource management lies the need to balance limited resources with the demands of the project. This includes assigning the right people to the right tasks, ensuring that equipment and materials are available when needed, and managing the project budget to prevent cost overruns. Traditionally, this has required project managers to make decisions based on their experience, intuition, and often incomplete data. While these methods can work, they are not always the most efficient or accurate.

AI changes the game by bringing a level of data-driven precision to resource management that was previously unattainable. By analyzing vast amounts of data, AI can identify patterns, predict needs, and make recommendations that optimize resource allocation. This not only reduces the likelihood of resource-related issues but also helps project managers make more informed decisions that improve project outcomes.

One of the key areas where AI enhances resource management is in the allocation of human resources. In any project, people are one of the most valuable and often most limited resources. Assigning the right team members to the right tasks is crucial for success. AI can assist in this process by analyzing data on team members' skills, past performance, and availability. For example, if a project requires a highly skilled developer to tackle a complex task, AI can identify the team member best suited for the job based on their experience and current workload.

Moreover, AI can help balance workloads across the team, ensuring that no one is overburdened while others are underutilized. This not only improves productivity but also enhances team morale by preventing burnout. By continuously monitoring team performance, AI can also identify potential issues, such as a team member falling behind on tasks or showing signs of fatigue, allowing the project manager to take corrective action before it impacts the project.

Another critical aspect of resource management is the availability of equipment and materials. In complex projects, delays in receiving materials or equipment can cause significant disruptions. AI can help mitigate these risks by predicting when resources will be needed and ensuring they are available at the right time. For example, by analyzing historical data and current project timelines, AI can forecast when specific materials will be required and trigger procurement processes well in advance. This reduces the risk of delays and ensures that the project continues to progress smoothly.

AI also plays a vital role in budget management, another crucial element of resource management. Keeping a project within budget is often one of the most challenging tasks for a project manager. Cost overruns can occur for a variety of reasons, from underestimating the time required for certain tasks to unexpected price increases for materials. AI can help project managers stay on top of the budget by providing real-time cost tracking and forecasting. By analyzing spending patterns and comparing them to the budget, AI can identify potential cost overruns before they occur, allowing the project manager to take corrective action.

For example, if AI detects that the project is spending more on materials than initially estimated, it can alert the project manager, who can then investigate the cause and make adjustments, such as renegotiating with suppliers or finding alternative materials. This proactive approach to budget management helps keep the project financially on track and reduces the risk of cost-related surprises.

Furthermore, AI can optimize resource utilization across multiple projects. In organizations where resources are shared across different projects, it's often challenging to ensure that each project gets what it needs without overcommitting resources. AI can analyze the demands of each project and suggest the most efficient allocation of resources across the portfolio. This helps prevent resource conflicts, reduces waste, and ensures that all projects have the resources they need to succeed.

AI's ability to manage resources extends beyond just people, materials, and money. Time is another critical resource in any project, and AI can help optimize how it is used. Time management in project management involves creating realistic schedules, tracking progress, and making adjustments as needed. AI can enhance this process by analyzing data on task durations, team performance, and external factors that could impact the schedule. For example, if AI detects that a particular task is taking longer than expected, it can automatically adjust the schedule and notify the project manager of the delay.

Additionally, AI can help project managers identify opportunities to save time by automating routine tasks. For example, AI can generate progress reports, send reminders, and update schedules automatically, freeing up the project manager to focus on more strategic activities. This not only improves efficiency but also helps ensure that the project stays on track.

In summary, AI-driven resource management offers a new level of precision and efficiency in project management. By leveraging AI's ability to analyze data, predict needs, and optimize resource allocation, project managers can make more informed decisions, reduce the risk of resource-related issues, and ultimately deliver better project outcomes. As AI continues to evolve, its role in resource management will likely expand, offering even more opportunities to enhance the way projects are managed.

However, it's important to remember that while AI can significantly improve resource management, it is not a replacement for human judgment. Project managers must still exercise their expertise and intuition, using AI as a tool to support, rather than replace, their decision-making. As we continue to explore the integration of AI into project management, understanding how to balance AI's capabilities with human oversight will be key to unlocking its full potential.

Part 2
Practical Applications of AI in Project Management

Chapter 5

Chapter 5

Enhancing Team Collaboration with AI

Team collaboration is at the heart of every successful project. No matter how well a project is planned or how efficiently resources are managed, the success of a project ultimately depends on the ability of the team to work together effectively. As projects become more complex and teams more dispersed, maintaining seamless collaboration becomes increasingly challenging. This is where artificial intelligence (AI) steps in, offering innovative solutions to enhance team collaboration, streamline communication, and ensure everyone is working towards the same goals. In this chapter, we'll explore how AI is transforming team collaboration in project management, helping teams stay connected, coordinated, and productive.

In traditional project management, team collaboration often relies on regular meetings, emails, and shared documents to keep everyone on the same page. While these methods can be effective, they are not without their limitations. Miscommunications, missed updates, and the challenges of coordinating across different time zones can all hinder collaboration. AI offers new tools and approaches that can overcome these challenges, making collaboration more efficient and effective.

One of the most significant ways AI enhances team collaboration is through intelligent communication tools. AI-powered platforms can facilitate real-time communication, ensuring that team members can stay connected no matter where they are located. These tools can automatically translate messages between different languages, allowing for seamless communication in global teams. Additionally, AI can summarize long discussions or meetings, highlighting key points and decisions, so everyone is up to speed without needing to go through lengthy transcripts or emails.

AI also plays a crucial role in ensuring that information is shared consistently and accurately across the team. In any project, it's vital that everyone has access to the most up-to-date information, whether it's the latest version of a document, the current project timeline, or recent changes to the scope of work. AI can help by automatically syncing documents, updating project dashboards, and notifying team members of important changes. This reduces the risk of errors or miscommunication and ensures that everyone is working with the same information.

In addition to enhancing communication, AI can also improve task coordination within the team. In complex projects, keeping track of who is doing what, when tasks are due, and how different tasks interconnect can be challenging. AI can assist by automatically assigning tasks based on team members' availability and expertise, setting deadlines, and sending reminders as due dates approach. For example, if a particular task is dependent on the completion of another, AI can ensure that the first task is completed on time and automatically notify the next team member when it's their turn to take over.

Furthermore, AI can help identify potential bottlenecks in the workflow before they become issues. By analyzing data on task progress, AI can detect when a task is falling behind or when a team member is overloaded with work. It can then suggest adjustments, such as redistributing tasks or extending deadlines, to keep the project on track. This proactive approach to task management helps prevent delays and ensures that the team can work efficiently.

Another area where AI enhances team collaboration is in decision-making. In project management, teams are often required to make collective decisions, whether it's choosing a course of action, resolving a conflict, or setting priorities. AI can support this process by providing data-driven insights and recommendations. For example, if the team needs to decide on the best approach to a problem, AI can analyze past project data, current market trends, and potential risks to suggest the most viable options. This not only speeds up the decision-making process but also helps ensure that decisions are based on solid information rather than guesswork.

AI can also facilitate better collaboration by offering predictive insights. For instance, AI can analyze team dynamics, such as communication patterns or past performance, to predict potential conflicts or collaboration challenges. If AI detects that a particular team member is becoming disengaged or that communication between certain team members is declining, it can alert the project manager, who can then take steps to address the issue. This predictive capability helps maintain a positive and productive team environment, where issues are addressed before they escalate.

Additionally, AI-powered tools can help teams collaborate more creatively and innovatively. For example, AI can generate ideas, suggest alternative approaches to a problem, or provide inspiration for new solutions. By analyzing data from previous projects, industry trends, or even social media, AI can offer insights that spark new ideas and encourage out-of-the-box thinking. This not only enhances the quality of the team's work but also fosters a culture of innovation and continuous improvement.

Moreover, AI can support remote collaboration, which has become increasingly important in today's globalized and digital work environment. Remote teams often face challenges in building rapport, maintaining communication, and staying aligned on goals. AI can help bridge these gaps by facilitating virtual meetings, monitoring team engagement, and providing tools that make remote collaboration as seamless as in-person teamwork. For example, AI can recommend the best times for meetings across different time zones, ensuring that everyone can participate without disruption.

However, while AI offers many benefits for team collaboration, it's essential to approach its integration thoughtfully. Collaboration is inherently human, and the success of AI in this area depends on its ability to enhance, rather than replace, human interaction. Project managers need to ensure that AI tools are used to support collaboration in ways that are meaningful and relevant to the team. This might involve training team members on how to use AI tools effectively, encouraging open communication about how AI is being used, and fostering a culture of trust where AI is seen as a partner rather than a threat.

In this chapter, we've explored how AI is enhancing team collaboration in project management. By improving communication, task coordination, decision-making, and remote work, AI is helping teams work together more effectively and efficiently. As AI continues to evolve, its role in team collaboration will likely expand, offering even more opportunities to enhance the way teams work together. Ultimately, by leveraging AI's capabilities, project managers can create a more connected, coordinated, and collaborative team environment, leading to better project outcomes and greater team satisfaction.

AI-Powered Project Management

Chapter 6

Chapter 6

AI in Risk Management

Risk management is a critical component of project management, essential for ensuring that projects are completed on time, within budget, and to the desired quality. Traditionally, risk management has relied on the experience and intuition of project managers, supported by tools and techniques such as risk registers, SWOT analysis, and contingency planning. While these methods can be effective, they are often limited by the complexity and unpredictability of modern projects. Artificial intelligence (AI) offers a new approach to risk management, providing advanced tools that can identify, assess, and mitigate risks more accurately and efficiently than ever before. In this chapter, we'll explore how AI is revolutionizing risk management in project management, helping teams navigate uncertainty and reduce the likelihood of project failures.

At its core, risk management involves identifying potential threats to the project, assessing their likelihood and impact, and developing strategies to mitigate or avoid them. This process can be challenging, particularly in complex projects where risks can emerge from a wide range of sources, including technical challenges, resource constraints, market fluctuations, and external events such as natural disasters or political instability. AI can enhance every stage of the risk management process, making it more proactive, data-driven, and responsive to change.

One of the most significant ways AI enhances risk management is through its ability to analyze large amounts of data to identify potential risks. Traditional risk identification often relies on brainstorming sessions, checklists, and past experience, which can lead to the oversight of less obvious risks. AI, on the other hand, can analyze data from a wide range of sources, including past projects, industry trends, market data, and even social media, to identify patterns and anomalies that could indicate potential risks. For example, AI might detect that a particular supplier has a history of delivery delays or that a specific technology has a high failure rate in similar projects. By providing early warnings, AI enables project managers to take proactive steps to address these risks before they impact the project.

AI's ability to assess risks is equally transformative. In traditional risk assessment, project managers typically estimate the likelihood and impact of each risk based on their judgment and available data. While this approach can be effective, it is inherently subjective and can be influenced by biases or incomplete information. AI can enhance risk assessment by providing more objective and data-driven insights. For instance, AI can use predictive analytics to assess the probability of various risks based on historical data, current trends, and project-specific factors. This allows for a more accurate and nuanced understanding of risks, enabling project managers to prioritize them more effectively.

Moreover, AI can help project managers assess the potential impact of risks more accurately. For example, by analyzing data from past projects, AI can estimate the likely cost, time, and quality implications of different risks. This can include assessing how a delay in one part of the project might cascade through the project schedule, or how a cost overrun in one area could affect the overall budget. By providing a clearer picture of the potential consequences of risks, AI enables project managers to develop more effective mitigation strategies.

Mitigating risks is another area where AI can make a significant difference. Traditional risk mitigation strategies often involve creating contingency plans, such as allocating extra time or budget for high-risk activities, or developing alternative plans in case of specific events. While these strategies are essential, they can be resource-intensive and may not always be sufficient to address emerging risks. AI can enhance risk mitigation by providing real-time monitoring and response capabilities. For example, AI can continuously monitor project data for signs of emerging risks, such as delays, cost overruns, or quality issues. If a risk is detected, AI can automatically trigger predefined mitigation actions, such as reallocating resources, adjusting the project schedule, or notifying the project manager.

AI can also support more dynamic and adaptive risk management. In complex projects, risks can evolve over time, with new risks emerging and existing risks changing in likelihood or impact. AI can help project managers stay ahead of these changes by providing continuous risk assessment and updating risk profiles as new data becomes available. For example, if a supplier's performance starts to decline, AI can update the risk assessment to reflect the increased likelihood of supply chain disruptions. This dynamic approach to risk management ensures that project managers can respond to risks in real-time, reducing the chances of project failure.

In addition to enhancing risk identification, assessment, and mitigation, AI can also improve the documentation and communication of risks. Effective risk management requires that all stakeholders are aware of the risks facing the project and understand the strategies in place to address them. AI can automate the creation of risk reports and dashboards, providing clear and up-to-date information on the status of risks. These reports can be customized for different stakeholders, ensuring that each person has the information they need to make informed decisions. For example, a project sponsor might receive a high-level summary of key risks and mitigation strategies, while team members might receive more detailed information on specific risks relevant to their tasks.

Moreover, AI can facilitate better communication and collaboration around risk management. For instance, AI-powered tools can enable project managers to share risk information with the team in real-time, fostering a culture of transparency and collective responsibility. AI can also help project teams collaborate on risk mitigation strategies by providing suggestions, generating alternative plans, and facilitating decision-making processes. This collaborative approach to risk management helps ensure that risks are addressed in a coordinated and comprehensive manner.

While AI offers significant benefits for risk management, it's important to recognize that it is not a silver bullet. AI tools are only as good as the data they rely on, and their effectiveness depends on how well they are integrated into the overall project management process. Project managers must still exercise their judgment and expertise, using AI as a tool to enhance, rather than replace, traditional risk management practices. Additionally, project managers must be aware of the limitations of AI, such as its potential for bias or its reliance on historical data, which may not always predict future risks accurately.

In this chapter, we've explored how AI is transforming risk management in project management. By enhancing risk identification, assessment, mitigation, and communication, AI enables project managers to manage risks more proactively, accurately, and efficiently. As AI continues to evolve, its role in risk management will likely expand, offering even more opportunities to reduce uncertainty and improve project outcomes. Ultimately, by leveraging AI's capabilities, project managers can create a more resilient and adaptive approach to risk management, ensuring that their projects are better equipped to handle the challenges and uncertainties of the modern world.

Chapter 7

Chapter 7

AI-Driven Decision Making in Project Management

Decision-making is at the heart of project management. Every project involves a continuous series of decisions, from setting initial goals and allocating resources to managing risks and adjusting plans as the project evolves. The quality of these decisions directly impacts the success of the project. Traditionally, decision-making in project management has relied on the experience, intuition, and judgment of project managers, supported by data and analytical tools. However, as projects become more complex and data-driven, the limitations of human decision-making are becoming more apparent. Artificial intelligence (AI) is revolutionizing decision-making in project management, providing advanced tools that can process vast amounts of data, identify patterns, and generate insights that help project managers make more informed and effective decisions. In this chapter, we will explore how AI is transforming decision-making in project management, making it more data-driven, accurate, and adaptive.

At the core of AI-driven decision-making is the ability to process and analyze large volumes of data in real-time. In traditional project management, decision-making is often constrained by the time and effort required to gather and analyze data. This can lead to delays in decision-making, reliance on incomplete or outdated information, and a tendency to make decisions based on intuition rather than evidence. AI overcomes these limitations by automating data collection and analysis, enabling project managers to access real-time insights that are based on the most current and comprehensive data available.

For example, consider a project manager faced with the decision of whether to proceed with a particular task that is running behind schedule. Traditionally, the project manager might rely on reports, meetings, and their own judgment to make this decision. However, with AI, the project manager can instantly access data on the current status of the task, the performance of the team members involved, the potential impact on the overall project timeline, and the availability of alternative resources. AI can analyze this data and provide a recommendation, such as whether to reallocate resources, adjust the schedule, or take other corrective actions. This allows the project manager to make a more informed decision that is grounded in data rather than guesswork.

AI's ability to generate predictive insights is another key factor in enhancing decision-making. Predictive analytics involves using historical data and statistical algorithms to forecast future outcomes. In project management, predictive analytics can be used to anticipate potential challenges, such as delays, cost overruns, or quality issues, before they occur. By identifying these risks early, AI enables project managers to take proactive measures to mitigate them, reducing the likelihood of project failure.

For instance, AI can analyze past project data to identify patterns that indicate potential delays, such as a certain type of task consistently taking longer than expected or a particular supplier frequently delivering materials late. By recognizing these patterns, AI can predict when similar issues are likely to occur in the current project and recommend preemptive actions, such as adjusting the project schedule, allocating additional resources, or selecting an alternative supplier. This predictive capability helps project managers stay ahead of potential problems and make decisions that keep the project on track.

AI can also enhance decision-making by providing scenario analysis and optimization tools. In complex projects, decision-making often involves evaluating multiple options and determining the best course of action. For example, a project manager might need to decide whether to invest in additional resources to accelerate a project or to extend the timeline to stay within budget. AI can assist in this process by simulating different scenarios and assessing the potential outcomes of each option. By comparing the costs, benefits, and risks associated with different choices, AI enables project managers to make decisions that optimize project outcomes.

Moreover, AI can support decision-making by providing recommendations that are tailored to the specific context of the project. In traditional project management, decision-making often relies on standardized approaches and best practices, which may not always be suitable for the unique challenges of a particular project. AI can overcome this limitation by analyzing the specific characteristics of the project, such as its goals, resources, and constraints, and generating recommendations that are customized to the project's needs. For example, if a project is operating under tight budget constraints, AI might recommend cost-saving measures that are most relevant to the project's industry or location.

In addition to enhancing individual decision-making, AI can also improve collective decision-making within project teams. In many projects, decisions are made collaboratively, involving input from multiple stakeholders, team members, and experts. AI can facilitate this process by providing a common platform for data sharing, analysis, and discussion. For example, AI-powered collaboration tools can enable team members to contribute their insights, assess different options, and reach consensus more efficiently. By providing a shared understanding of the data and the potential implications of different decisions, AI helps ensure that collective decisions are well-informed and aligned with the project's goals.

AI can also play a role in automating routine decisions, freeing up project managers to focus on more strategic tasks. In any project, there are numerous routine decisions that need to be made, such as approving expenses, assigning tasks, or updating schedules. While these decisions are important, they can be time-consuming and distract project managers from more critical activities. AI can automate many of these routine decisions by applying predefined rules, algorithms, and criteria. For example, AI can automatically approve expenses that fall within a certain budget range or assign tasks to team members based on their availability and skills. By automating these routine decisions, AI allows project managers to focus on higher-level decision-making that requires their expertise and judgment.

While AI offers significant benefits for decision-making in project management, it's important to recognize that AI is not a replacement for human judgment. Decision-making in project management often involves complex trade-offs, ethical considerations, and the need to balance competing priorities. These aspects of decision-making require human intuition, experience, and creativity, which AI cannot replicate. Instead, AI should be seen as a tool that enhances and supports human decision-making, providing data-driven insights and recommendations that help project managers make better decisions.

In this chapter, we've explored how AI is transforming decision-making in project management. By automating data analysis, providing predictive insights, optimizing decision scenarios, and supporting collective decision-making, AI enables project managers to make more informed, accurate, and timely decisions. As AI continues to evolve, its role in decision-making will likely expand, offering even more opportunities to enhance the quality and effectiveness of decisions in project management. Ultimately, by leveraging AI's capabilities, project managers can make smarter decisions that lead to better project outcomes, helping them achieve their goals and deliver successful projects in an increasingly complex and dynamic environment.

Chapter 8

Chapter 8

Enhancing Communication and Collaboration with AI

Effective communication and collaboration are the lifeblood of successful project management. Every project relies on the seamless exchange of information, ideas, and feedback among team members, stakeholders, and clients. However, as teams become more diverse, geographically dispersed, and reliant on digital tools, maintaining clear and efficient communication can be increasingly challenging. Misunderstandings, delays, and information silos can lead to costly errors and project failures. Artificial intelligence (AI) offers new solutions to these challenges, providing advanced tools that enhance communication and foster collaboration across project teams. In this chapter, we'll explore how AI is transforming the way project teams communicate and work together, creating more cohesive, productive, and successful projects.

One of the most significant ways AI enhances communication in project management is through intelligent automation and real-time data processing. Traditional communication in projects often relies on scheduled meetings, emails, and reports, which can lead to delays in the dissemination of information. Important updates may be missed, and decisions may be based on outdated data. AI-powered communication tools, on the other hand, can automatically process and distribute information in real-time, ensuring that everyone on the team has access to the most current and relevant data. For example, AI can monitor project progress, detect changes or issues, and instantly notify the appropriate team members, eliminating the need to wait for the next meeting or report.

In addition to real-time updates, AI can also facilitate more personalized and context-aware communication. In many projects, team members have different roles, responsibilities, and areas of expertise, which means they need access to different types of information. AI can analyze the specific needs and preferences of each team member and deliver tailored communication that is relevant to their role. For instance, a project manager might receive a high-level overview of project progress and risks, while a developer might receive detailed technical updates on the tasks they are working on. This personalized approach to communication helps ensure that team members have the information they need to do their jobs effectively, without being overwhelmed by irrelevant details.

AI can also enhance communication by improving the clarity and effectiveness of messages. Miscommunication is a common problem in project management, often leading to misunderstandings, errors, and rework. AI-powered language processing tools can help mitigate these risks by analyzing the clarity, tone, and intent of messages before they are sent. For example, AI can identify ambiguous language, suggest clearer alternatives, and ensure that the tone of the message is appropriate for the audience. This helps prevent miscommunication and ensures that messages are understood as intended.

Moreover, AI can facilitate communication across different languages and cultures, which is particularly important in global projects involving diverse teams. Language barriers can hinder collaboration and lead to misunderstandings, but AI-powered translation tools can automatically translate messages, documents, and reports in real-time, allowing team members to communicate effectively regardless of their native language. Additionally, AI can analyze cultural differences and provide guidance on how to communicate in a way that is respectful and effective across different cultural contexts. This cultural sensitivity enhances collaboration and helps build trust among team members from different backgrounds.

Collaboration is another area where AI is making a significant impact. Traditional collaboration often relies on manual coordination, with team members needing to schedule meetings, share documents, and coordinate tasks through various channels. This can be time-consuming and prone to errors, particularly in large or complex projects. AI-powered collaboration tools can automate many of these processes, streamlining the way teams work together. For example, AI can automatically schedule meetings based on team members' availability, assign tasks based on their skills and workload, and track progress to ensure that deadlines are met. By reducing the administrative burden of collaboration, AI allows teams to focus on the creative and strategic aspects of their work.

AI can also enhance collaboration by providing intelligent insights and recommendations. In many projects, collaboration involves brainstorming, problem-solving, and decision-making, which require input from multiple team members. AI can support these processes by analyzing data, identifying patterns, and generating insights that help teams make better decisions. For example, AI might analyze project data to identify potential bottlenecks or suggest alternative approaches to a problem. These insights can be shared with the team in real-time, facilitating more informed and productive discussions.

Furthermore, AI can help break down information silos and foster cross-functional collaboration. In large organizations or complex projects, different teams or departments may have their own systems, processes, and data, which can lead to silos where information is not easily shared. AI can integrate data from different sources, providing a unified view of the project that is accessible to all team members. This helps ensure that everyone is working from the same set of information and reduces the risk of duplication or conflict. By breaking down silos, AI enables more effective collaboration across different functions and disciplines, leading to better project outcomes.

AI can also play a role in fostering a collaborative culture within project teams. Collaboration is not just about tools and processes; it also requires a mindset of openness, trust, and shared responsibility. AI can support this by providing feedback and insights that encourage positive collaboration behaviors. For example, AI can analyze team interactions to identify patterns of communication, such as who speaks the most in meetings or who is frequently left out of discussions. Based on this analysis, AI can provide recommendations for more inclusive and balanced collaboration, such as encouraging quieter team members to contribute or ensuring that all voices are heard. This helps create a more collaborative and supportive team environment, where everyone feels valued and engaged.

In addition to enhancing communication and collaboration within project teams, AI can also improve the way teams interact with stakeholders. Stakeholder communication is a critical aspect of project management, as it ensures that clients, sponsors, and other external parties are kept informed and engaged throughout the project. AI can support stakeholder communication by automating the creation of reports, dashboards, and updates, ensuring that stakeholders receive accurate and timely information. AI can also analyze stakeholder feedback and sentiment, providing insights that help project managers address concerns and maintain positive relationships.

While AI offers significant benefits for communication and collaboration in project management, it's important to recognize that it should be used as a tool to support, rather than replace, human interaction. Communication and collaboration are inherently human activities that involve not only the exchange of information but also the building of relationships, trust, and understanding. AI can enhance these activities by providing tools and insights that make them more efficient and effective, but it cannot replace the empathy, creativity, and emotional intelligence that are essential for successful collaboration.

In this chapter, we've explored how AI is transforming communication and collaboration in project management. By automating data processing, personalizing communication, enhancing clarity, and fostering cross-functional collaboration, AI enables project teams to work together more effectively and achieve better outcomes. As AI continues to evolve, its role in communication and collaboration will likely expand, offering even more opportunities to enhance the way teams interact and work together. Ultimately, by leveraging AI's capabilities, project managers can create more cohesive, engaged, and high-performing teams that are better equipped to succeed in today's complex and dynamic project environments.

AI-Powered Project Management

Chapter 9

Chapter 9

AI-Enhanced Risk Management and Mitigation

Risk management is a fundamental aspect of project management, playing a critical role in the success of any project. Every project, regardless of its size or complexity, is fraught with uncertainties and potential challenges that can derail progress or lead to failure. Traditionally, risk management involves identifying potential risks, assessing their impact, and developing strategies to mitigate or avoid them. While this approach has proven effective, it is often limited by the availability of data, the accuracy of predictions, and the ability of project managers to foresee all possible risks.

Artificial intelligence (AI) is revolutionizing risk management by providing advanced tools and techniques that enhance the identification, assessment, and mitigation of risks. In this chapter, we will explore how AI is transforming risk management in project management, making it more proactive, precise, and adaptive.

At the heart of AI-enhanced risk management is the ability to analyze vast amounts of data to identify potential risks that might not be immediately apparent. Traditional risk management often relies on historical data, expert judgment, and qualitative assessments to identify risks. While these methods are valuable, they can miss emerging risks or fail to recognize patterns that are not obvious. AI, on the other hand, can process and analyze data from a wide range of sources, including historical project data, real-time performance metrics, market trends, and external factors such as economic or geopolitical events. By leveraging machine learning algorithms and predictive analytics, AI can identify subtle patterns and correlations that indicate potential risks, even those that may not have occurred in previous projects.

For example, AI might analyze a project's progress and detect early signs of schedule slippage, such as a consistent delay in task completion times or a drop in team productivity. Based on this analysis, AI can flag the risk of a potential delay and recommend actions to mitigate it, such as reallocating resources, adjusting deadlines, or addressing team morale. This proactive approach to risk identification allows project managers to address issues before they escalate, reducing the likelihood of costly delays or project failure.

AI also enhances the assessment of risks by providing more accurate and dynamic risk models. Traditional risk assessment often involves estimating the likelihood and impact of risks based on static models or past experiences. While these estimates can be useful, they are inherently limited by the assumptions and data used to create them. AI can improve the accuracy of risk assessments by continuously updating risk models based on real-time data and feedback. For instance, as a project progresses, AI can monitor key performance indicators (KPIs), such as budget adherence, resource utilization, and stakeholder satisfaction, and adjust risk assessments accordingly. This dynamic risk modeling allows project managers to make more informed decisions and allocate resources more effectively to mitigate risks.

Moreover, AI can provide a more nuanced understanding of the interdependencies and cascading effects of risks. In complex projects, risks are often interconnected, meaning that the occurrence of one risk can trigger or exacerbate others. Traditional risk management approaches may not fully capture these interdependencies, leading to an incomplete or overly simplistic view of project risks. AI, however, can analyze the relationships between different risks and predict how they might interact. For example, AI might identify that a delay in the delivery of a key component could lead to cost overruns due to the need for expedited shipping, which in turn could affect the overall project budget and stakeholder confidence. By understanding these interdependencies, AI enables project managers to develop more comprehensive risk mitigation strategies that address the root causes and potential ripple effects of risks.

In addition to identifying and assessing risks, AI plays a crucial role in risk mitigation by providing intelligent recommendations and automating routine risk management tasks. In traditional risk management, the development of mitigation strategies often relies on the experience and judgment of project managers, supported by risk management tools and frameworks. While these strategies can be effective, they may not always be tailored to the specific context of the project or take into account the latest data. AI can enhance risk mitigation by generating recommendations that are based on a deep analysis of the project's unique characteristics, as well as best practices from similar projects. For example, AI might suggest specific contingency plans, resource reallocation strategies, or changes to the project schedule that are most likely to mitigate identified risks.

AI can also automate many routine aspects of risk management, freeing up project managers to focus on more strategic tasks. For instance, AI can automatically monitor project data for early warning signs of risks, generate risk reports, and track the implementation of mitigation measures. By automating these tasks, AI reduces the administrative burden on project managers and ensures that risks are managed consistently and effectively throughout the project lifecycle.

Furthermore, AI can enhance risk communication and stakeholder management by providing clear and actionable insights into project risks. Effective communication of risks is essential for ensuring that all stakeholders understand the potential challenges and are aligned on the strategies to address them. However, traditional risk communication can be hampered by the complexity of risk data and the difficulty of conveying it in a way that is meaningful to nonexperts. AI can simplify risk communication by generating visualizations, summaries, and recommendations that are easy to understand and tailored to the needs of different stakeholders. For example, AI might create a dashboard that provides an at-a-glance overview of the top risks facing the project, along with the status of mitigation measures and the potential impact on project outcomes. This transparency helps build trust with stakeholders and ensures that everyone is on the same page regarding the project's risk profile.

In addition to its role in managing project-specific risks, AI can also help organizations build a more resilient approach to risk management at the portfolio or enterprise level. By analyzing data across multiple projects, AI can identify trends, common risk factors, and emerging threats that may affect the organization as a whole. For example, AI might detect that a certain type of project consistently experiences delays due to supplier issues, prompting the organization to review and strengthen its supplier management processes. This broader perspective on risk management enables organizations to learn from past experiences, improve their risk management practices, and better prepare for future challenges.

While AI offers significant advantages for risk management in project management, it's important to recognize that it is not a silver bullet. Risk management still requires human judgment, experience, and creativity, particularly when dealing with complex or unprecedented risks. AI should be seen as a powerful tool that enhances and supports the risk management process, providing data-driven insights and recommendations that help project managers make more informed decisions. By combining the strengths of AI with the expertise of project managers, organizations can achieve a more proactive, precise, and adaptive approach to risk management.

In this chapter, we've explored how AI is transforming risk management in project management. By enhancing risk identification, assessment, and mitigation, AI enables project managers to manage risks more effectively and increase the likelihood of project success. As AI continues to evolve, its role in risk management will likely expand, offering even more opportunities to improve the way risks are managed in projects. Ultimately, by leveraging AI's capabilities, project managers can create more resilient and successful projects that are better equipped to navigate the uncertainties and challenges of today's dynamic project environment.

Part 3
Challenges and Ethical Considerations

Chapter 10

Chapter 10

AI in Resource Allocation and Optimization

Effective resource allocation is a cornerstone of successful project management. Whether it's assigning team members to tasks, managing budgets, or scheduling equipment, the ability to allocate resources efficiently can significantly impact a project's success. However, resource management is often fraught with challenges, from balancing competing demands to responding to unexpected changes. Traditional approaches to resource allocation rely heavily on project managers' experience, intuition, and manual processes, which can be time-consuming and prone to errors. Artificial intelligence (AI) is transforming resource allocation and optimization by providing advanced tools that enable project managers to make data-driven decisions, maximize resource efficiency, and adapt to changing project conditions with greater agility. In this chapter, we will explore how AI is revolutionizing resource management in project management, leading to more successful and cost-effective projects.

One of the primary ways AI enhances resource allocation is through its ability to analyze vast amounts of data and identify patterns that might not be immediately apparent to human project managers. Traditional resource allocation often involves manually matching resources to tasks based on availability, skills, and experience. While this approach can be effective, it may overlook subtle factors that could affect the success of the allocation, such as individual productivity trends, past performance in similar tasks, or the interdependencies between tasks. AI, powered by machine learning algorithms, can analyze historical project data, real-time performance metrics, and other relevant information to generate more accurate and optimized resource allocation plans. For instance, AI might identify that a particular team member consistently performs better when working on tasks that require creative problem-solving, or that certain resources are more likely to be available during specific periods. By leveraging these insights, AI can suggest the optimal allocation of resources to maximize productivity and minimize the risk of delays or bottlenecks.

In addition to optimizing the allocation of human resources, AI can also enhance the management of non-human resources, such as equipment, materials, and budgets. In many projects, managing these resources involves complex trade-offs and decisions, such as balancing the cost of expedited shipping against the risk of missing a deadline, or deciding whether to rent or purchase equipment based on usage patterns. AI can analyze these trade-offs in real-time, considering factors such as cost, availability, and project impact to recommend the most cost-effective and efficient resource management strategies. For example, AI might suggest renting equipment for a short-term project where usage is intermittent, while recommending purchasing equipment for a long-term project where continuous use is expected. By optimizing these decisions, AI helps project managers reduce costs and ensure that resources are used in the most efficient way possible.

Another key advantage of AI in resource management is its ability to dynamically adjust resource allocation in response to changing project conditions. In traditional resource management, once resources are allocated, any changes to the project plan, such as scope adjustments or unexpected delays, require manual intervention to reallocate resources. This can be a time-consuming and error-prone process, particularly in large or complex projects. AI, however, can continuously monitor project progress, performance metrics, and external factors, and automatically adjust resource allocation as needed. For example, if a task is taking longer than expected to complete, AI can reassign additional team members to help, or if a critical piece of equipment becomes unavailable, AI can suggest alternative resources or schedule adjustments. This dynamic resource allocation ensures that projects remain on track and that resources are used effectively even in the face of unexpected challenges.

AI can also enhance the strategic aspect of resource management by providing project managers with intelligent insights and recommendations that go beyond immediate operational decisions. For instance, AI can analyze data across multiple projects to identify trends and patterns that can inform long-term resource planning and strategy. This might include insights into which skills are in high demand across projects, which resources are consistently over- or under-utilized, or how changes in market conditions are likely to impact future resource needs. Armed with these insights, project managers can make more informed decisions about resource acquisition, training and development, and capacity planning, ensuring that their organizations are well-positioned to meet future project demands.

Moreover, AI can support project managers in making more equitable and transparent resource allocation decisions. In many organizations, resource allocation can be influenced by subjective factors, such as personal preferences, office politics, or unconscious biases. This can lead to uneven workloads, underutilization of certain team members, or a lack of diversity in project teams. AI, by providing objective data-driven recommendations, can help reduce these biases and ensure that resources are allocated based on merit, skills, and project needs rather than personal or political considerations. For example, AI might highlight that a junior team member has the right skills and availability for a task that would typically be assigned to a more senior colleague, thereby providing opportunities for growth and development across the team. By promoting fairness and transparency in resource allocation, AI helps create a more inclusive and effective project management environment.

AI's role in resource optimization also extends to the broader organizational level, where it can help align resource management with overall business goals and strategies. For example, AI can analyze the alignment between resource allocation decisions and strategic objectives, such as maximizing return on investment (ROI), supporting innovation, or improving customer satisfaction. If AI identifies that certain projects or tasks are not aligned with these objectives, it can recommend reallocating resources to more strategically important areas. This ensures that the organization's resources are used in a way that supports its long-term goals, rather than being driven solely by the immediate demands of individual projects.

Another important aspect of AI-enhanced resource management is its ability to support project managers in scenarios where resources are constrained or must be shared across multiple projects. In such situations, optimizing resource allocation can be particularly challenging, as it involves balancing competing priorities and managing potential conflicts between projects. AI can provide project managers with a more comprehensive view of resource availability and utilization across the organization, allowing them to make more informed decisions about how to allocate limited resources. For instance, AI might identify opportunities for resource sharing or collaboration between projects, or suggest prioritizing certain tasks or projects based on their strategic importance. This holistic approach to resource management helps ensure that resources are allocated in the most effective and efficient way possible, even in the face of constraints.

In addition to the practical benefits of AI in resource allocation and optimization, it's also important to consider the potential challenges and limitations. For example, while AI can provide valuable data-driven insights, it is still reliant on the quality and completeness of the data it is fed. Inaccurate or incomplete data can lead to suboptimal recommendations or decisions. Additionally, while AI can automate many aspects of resource management, it cannot replace the need for human judgment, creativity, and empathy, particularly in complex or high-stakes situations. Project managers must therefore be mindful of the need to balance AI-driven insights with their own experience and expertise.

In this chapter, we've explored how AI is transforming resource allocation and optimization in project management. By analyzing data, providing intelligent recommendations, and dynamically adjusting resource allocation, AI enables project managers to make more informed, efficient, and strategic decisions about how to allocate resources. As AI continues to evolve, its role in resource management is likely to expand, offering even more opportunities to optimize the way resources are managed in projects. Ultimately, by leveraging AI's capabilities, project managers can achieve better project outcomes, reduce costs, and ensure that resources are used in a way that aligns with both project and organizational goals.

Chapter 11

Chapter 11

AI-Driven Insights for Strategic Decision-Making

Strategic decision-making is a crucial aspect of project management, influencing not only the immediate course of a project but also its long-term success and alignment with organizational goals. Effective strategic decisions require a deep understanding of project dynamics, market conditions, and future trends. Traditionally, project managers have relied on their experience, intuition, and historical data to guide their decisions. However, the complexity and pace of modern projects often demand more sophisticated tools to ensure that decisions are both timely and informed. Artificial intelligence (AI) offers powerful capabilities to enhance strategic decision-making by providing advanced data analysis, predictive insights, and actionable recommendations. In this chapter, we will explore how AI is transforming strategic decision-making in project management, enabling project managers to make more informed, data-driven choices that align with their goals and drive project success.

One of the key ways AI enhances strategic decision-making is through its ability to analyze vast amounts of data and identify patterns that may not be readily apparent. In traditional project management, decision-making is often based on limited data or anecdotal evidence, which can lead to suboptimal choices or missed opportunities. AI, powered by machine learning algorithms and advanced analytics, can process large datasets from various sources—such as project performance metrics, market trends, and historical data—to uncover hidden patterns and trends. For example, AI might analyze data from multiple projects to identify factors that consistently lead to success or failure, providing project managers with valuable insights into what strategies are most effective. By leveraging these data-driven insights, project managers can make more informed decisions that are grounded in evidence rather than guesswork.

AI can also enhance strategic decision-making by providing predictive insights that help project managers anticipate future outcomes and plan accordingly. Predictive analytics, a subset of AI, involves using historical data and statistical models to forecast future trends and potential scenarios. For instance, AI can analyze past project performance to predict future risks, budget overruns, or schedule delays. This allows project managers to proactively address potential issues before they become critical, such as by adjusting project plans, reallocating resources, or implementing contingency measures. By providing a forward-looking perspective, AI enables project managers to make strategic decisions that are not only reactive but also proactive, positioning their projects for long-term success.

Another important aspect of AI-driven strategic decision-making is its ability to generate actionable recommendations based on data analysis. While data and insights are valuable, they are most effective when translated into specific actions that can be implemented to achieve desired outcomes. AI can analyze data from various sources and generate recommendations that are tailored to the project's unique context and goals. For example, if AI identifies a potential risk of budget overruns, it might recommend specific cost-saving measures or alternative approaches to mitigate the risk.

Similarly, if AI detects a trend in market demand, it might suggest adjustments to the project's scope or strategy to better align with customer needs. These actionable recommendations help project managers make decisions that are not only informed but also practical and effective in achieving project objectives.

AI can also support strategic decision-making by providing real-time insights and adaptive recommendations. Traditional decision-making processes often rely on periodic reviews and updates, which can result in delays and missed opportunities. AI, however, can continuously monitor project data and external factors, providing real-time insights and recommendations as conditions change. For example, AI might track market trends, competitor activities, or project performance metrics and adjust its recommendations accordingly. This real-time adaptability ensures that project managers have up-to-date information and guidance, allowing them to make decisions that are responsive to current conditions and emerging trends.

In addition to enhancing individual decision-making, AI can also support strategic decision-making at the organizational level by providing a comprehensive view of project performance and alignment with strategic goals. AI can aggregate data from multiple projects and analyze it to assess how well each project contributes to the organization's overall objectives. For example, AI might analyze project outcomes, resource utilization, and strategic alignment to identify which projects are delivering the highest value or contributing most effectively to business goals. This holistic view enables organizations to prioritize projects, allocate resources more effectively, and ensure that their project portfolio aligns with strategic priorities.

AI can also facilitate scenario planning and simulation, which are critical for strategic decision-making in complex and uncertain environments. Scenario planning involves exploring different potential future scenarios and assessing their impact on project outcomes and organizational goals. AI can simulate various scenarios based on different inputs and assumptions, providing project managers with insights into how different decisions or changes might affect the project's success. For example, AI might simulate the impact of changes in market conditions, resource availability, or project scope on project outcomes, helping project managers evaluate the potential risks and benefits of different strategies. This ability to model and explore different scenarios enhances decision-making by providing a clearer understanding of potential outcomes and trade-offs.

Moreover, AI can support strategic decision-making by enhancing collaboration and communication among project stakeholders. Effective decision-making often requires input from multiple stakeholders, including team members, clients, and executives. AI can facilitate this process by providing tools for data sharing, collaboration, and consensus-building. For example, AI-powered platforms can aggregate and visualize data from different stakeholders, enabling more informed discussions and collaborative decision-making. AI can also analyze stakeholder feedback and sentiment, providing insights into stakeholder concerns and preferences that can inform strategic decisions. This collaborative approach ensures that decisions are well-informed and aligned with the needs and expectations of all relevant parties.

Despite the many benefits of AI in strategic decision-making, it is important to recognize its limitations and challenges. AI is only as good as the data it is provided, and inaccurate or incomplete data can lead to suboptimal recommendations. Additionally, while AI can provide valuable insights and recommendations, it cannot replace the need for human judgment, creativity, and experience. Strategic decision-making often involves complex considerations, ethical dilemmas, and contextual factors that require human input and expertise. Therefore, project managers should use AI as a tool to enhance, rather than replace, their own decision-making processes.

In this chapter, we've explored how AI is transforming strategic decision-making in project management. By providing advanced data analysis, predictive insights, and actionable recommendations, AI enables project managers to make more informed, data-driven decisions that align with their goals and drive project success. As AI continues to evolve, its role in strategic decision-making is likely to expand, offering even more opportunities to enhance the way decisions are made in projects. Ultimately, by leveraging AI's capabilities, project managers can achieve better project outcomes, align with organizational objectives, and navigate the complexities of today's dynamic project environments with greater confidence and success.

Chapter 12

Chapter 12

AI for Enhancing Communication and Collaboration

Effective communication and collaboration are vital for the success of any project. They ensure that team members are aligned, stakeholders are informed, and project goals are achieved efficiently. However, managing communication and collaboration in projects can be challenging, especially in complex environments with diverse teams, multiple stakeholders, and varying communication channels. Traditional approaches to communication often involve meetings, emails, and manual tracking, which can be time-consuming and prone to errors. Artificial intelligence (AI) offers transformative capabilities to enhance communication and collaboration by streamlining processes, providing real-time insights, and facilitating more effective interactions. In this chapter, we will explore how AI is revolutionizing communication and collaboration in project management, leading to improved team dynamics, better information sharing, and more successful project outcomes.

One of the primary ways AI enhances communication is by automating routine tasks and reducing the administrative burden on project teams. For instance, AI-powered chatbots and virtual assistants can handle repetitive tasks such as scheduling meetings, sending reminders, and managing emails. By automating these tasks, AI frees up time for project managers and team members to focus on more strategic activities and reduces the risk of human error. For example, an AI chatbot might automatically schedule meetings based on participants' availability, send out agenda items, and follow up with action items, ensuring that communication flows smoothly without manual intervention.

AI can also improve communication by providing real-time language translation and transcription services. In global projects with team members from different linguistic backgrounds, language

AI-Powered Project Management

barriers can hinder effective communication. AI-powered translation tools can translate messages, documents, and meeting discussions in real-time, enabling seamless communication across language differences. Similarly, AI transcription services can convert spoken conversations into written text, making it easier for team members to review and refer back to important discussions. These tools help ensure that all team members are on the same page and can access critical information, regardless of their language or location.

Another significant benefit of AI in communication is its ability to analyze and summarize large volumes of information. In projects with extensive documentation, meeting notes, and communication threads, it can be challenging to keep track of key points and decisions. AI-powered summarization tools can analyze and condense lengthy documents, emails, and meeting notes into concise summaries, highlighting the most important information. For example, an AI tool might generate a summary of a project meeting, capturing key decisions, action items, and deadlines, making it easier for team members to stay informed and aligned. This capability helps improve information management and ensures that important details are not overlooked.

AI also enhances collaboration by providing advanced tools for virtual teamwork and interaction. In the era of remote and hybrid work, effective collaboration relies on technology that supports seamless communication and coordination among team members. AI-powered collaboration platforms can offer features such as real-time document editing, project management dashboards, and integrated communication channels. These platforms enable team members to work together more efficiently, share updates, and track progress in a centralized environment. For example, AI might analyze project data to provide insights into team performance, identify bottlenecks, and suggest ways to improve collaboration. This integrated approach helps ensure that team members are working together effectively and can access the information they need to contribute to the project's success.

Furthermore, AI can support collaboration by facilitating more effective decision-making and problem-solving. In collaborative environments, decision-making often involves input from multiple stakeholders and requires balancing different perspectives and priorities. AI can analyze data from various sources, such as stakeholder feedback, project performance metrics, and market trends, to provide insights that inform collaborative decision-making. For instance, AI might analyze feedback from team members and stakeholders to identify common concerns or preferences, helping to guide decisions that address the needs of all parties involved. By providing data-driven insights, AI helps ensure that collaborative decisions are based on a comprehensive understanding of the project's context and requirements.

AI can also enhance team dynamics and interpersonal relationships by providing tools for sentiment analysis and feedback. Understanding team members' emotions and sentiments can be crucial for maintaining a positive and productive work environment. AI-powered sentiment analysis tools can analyze communication data, such as emails and messages, to gauge team members' feelings and attitudes. For example, if AI detects a decline in team morale or increased frustration in communication patterns, it can alert project managers to potential issues and recommend strategies for addressing them. This proactive approach helps maintain a healthy team dynamic and supports effective collaboration.

Additionally, AI can improve collaboration by providing personalized recommendations and insights for individual team members. AI can analyze each team member's work patterns, preferences, and interactions to offer tailored suggestions that enhance their collaboration experience. For instance, AI might recommend specific team members to collaborate with based on their expertise and past interactions, or suggest optimal times for meetings based on individual schedules. These personalized recommendations help ensure that collaboration is efficient and effective, taking into account the unique needs and preferences of each team member.

Despite its many advantages, the integration of AI into communication and collaboration processes must be approached thoughtfully. While AI can enhance efficiency and effectiveness, it is essential to balance technology with human interaction and empathy. AI should be used as a tool to support and augment human communication, not replace it. Effective communication and collaboration still rely on interpersonal skills, emotional intelligence, and the ability to build trust and rapport among team members. Therefore, project managers should use AI to enhance their communication strategies while maintaining a focus on the human aspects of teamwork.

In this chapter, we've explored how AI is transforming communication and collaboration in project management. By automating routine tasks, providing real-time translation and transcription, summarizing information, and offering advanced collaboration tools, AI enhances the efficiency and effectiveness of communication processes. Additionally, AI supports collaborative decision-making, improves team dynamics, and offers personalized recommendations for individual team members. As AI continues to evolve, its role in communication and collaboration is likely to expand, offering even more opportunities to improve how teams work together and achieve project success. Ultimately, by leveraging AI's capabilities, project managers can create more cohesive, informed, and productive teams that are better equipped to navigate the complexities of modern projects.

Part 4

The Future of AI in Project Management

Chapter 13

Chapter 13

AI for Risk Management and Mitigation

Risk management is a fundamental aspect of project management, involving the identification, assessment, and mitigation of potential risks that could impact the success of a project. Effective risk management helps ensure that projects are completed on time, within budget, and to the desired quality standards. Traditional risk management processes often rely on manual assessments, historical data, and expert judgment to identify and address risks. However, the complexity and uncertainty of modern projects can make this process challenging and prone to oversight. Artificial intelligence (AI) is transforming risk management by providing advanced tools and techniques to better predict, assess, and mitigate risks. In this chapter, we will explore how AI is revolutionizing risk management in project management, enabling project managers to proactively address risks and enhance project outcomes.

One of the primary ways AI enhances risk management is through its ability to analyze large volumes of data and identify potential risks more accurately. Traditional risk management often involves reviewing historical data, expert opinions, and project documentation to identify risks. While this approach can be effective, it may not capture all potential risks, especially those that are complex or emerging. AI, powered by machine learning algorithms and advanced analytics, can analyze vast amounts of data from various sources, including project performance metrics, market trends, and historical records, to identify patterns and anomalies that may indicate potential risks. For example, AI might analyze data from previous projects to identify risk factors that were not initially apparent, such as specific project conditions or resource constraints that contributed to issues. By leveraging these insights, project managers can identify risks more comprehensively and take proactive measures to address them.

AI also enhances risk assessment by providing predictive insights that help project managers anticipate and quantify potential risks. Predictive analytics, a subset of AI, involves using historical data and statistical models to forecast future outcomes and assess the likelihood and impact of risks. For instance, AI can analyze past project data to predict the probability of schedule delays, budget overruns, or quality issues based on current project conditions. This allows project managers to assess the potential impact of risks on project objectives and make more informed decisions about risk mitigation strategies. For example, if AI predicts a high likelihood of budget overruns due to specific project variables, project managers can implement cost control measures or adjust project plans to mitigate the risk.

Another important aspect of AI in risk management is its ability to provide real-time monitoring and early warning systems. Traditional risk management often involves periodic reviews and updates, which can result in delays in identifying and addressing emerging risks. AI can continuously monitor project data, performance metrics, and external factors to provide real-time insights and alerts about potential risks. For example, AI might track changes in project performance indicators, such as delays in task completion or deviations from budget, and generate alerts when these indicators suggest potential risks. This real-time monitoring enables project managers to respond quickly to emerging issues and take corrective actions before risks escalate.

AI can also support risk mitigation by providing recommendations and simulations for different risk scenarios. In risk management, it is crucial to evaluate and implement effective mitigation strategies to address identified risks. AI can simulate various risk scenarios based on different inputs and assumptions, helping project managers evaluate the potential effectiveness of different mitigation strategies. For example, if AI identifies a risk of schedule delays due to resource constraints, it might simulate different resource allocation strategies to determine which approach would be most effective in minimizing the impact of the risk. These simulations help project managers make data-driven decisions about risk mitigation and ensure that their strategies are well-informed and effective.

Additionally, AI can enhance risk management by analyzing and learning from past risk events to improve future risk assessments. Machine learning algorithms can analyze historical risk data and outcomes to identify patterns and trends that can inform future risk management efforts. For instance, AI might analyze past projects to identify common risk factors or patterns that were associated with project failures or challenges. By understanding these patterns, project managers can improve their risk assessment processes and develop more effective risk management strategies for future projects. This continuous learning approach helps ensure that risk management practices evolve and adapt based on real-world experiences.

AI can also support risk communication and documentation by providing tools for capturing and sharing risk-related information. Effective risk management requires clear communication and documentation of risks, their potential impacts, and the strategies for addressing them. AI-powered tools can assist in documenting and organizing risk information, generating risk reports, and facilitating communication among project stakeholders. For example, AI might automatically generate risk reports based on real-time data and updates, providing stakeholders with timely and accurate information about risk status and mitigation efforts. This helps ensure that all stakeholders are informed and aligned regarding risk management activities.

Despite the many benefits of AI in risk management, it is important to consider its limitations and challenges. AI's effectiveness in risk management depends on the quality and completeness of the data it analyzes. Inaccurate or incomplete data can lead to misleading insights or recommendations. Additionally, while AI can provide valuable data-driven insights, it cannot replace the need for human judgment and expertise in assessing and addressing risks. Project managers must use AI as a tool to support their risk management efforts, while also applying their own experience and intuition to make informed decisions. Balancing AI-driven insights with human expertise ensures that risk management practices are both data-informed and contextually relevant.

In this chapter, we've explored how AI is transforming risk management in project management. By analyzing data, providing predictive insights, enabling real-time monitoring, and offering simulations for risk scenarios, AI enhances the ability to identify, assess, and mitigate risks more effectively. AI also supports risk communication and documentation, helping project managers stay informed and aligned with stakeholders. As AI continues to advance, its role in risk management is likely to expand, offering even more opportunities to improve how risks are managed in projects. Ultimately, by leveraging AI's capabilities, project managers can proactively address risks, enhance project outcomes, and navigate the complexities of modern projects with greater confidence and success.

Chapter 14

Chapter 14

AI in Project Resource Management

Effective resource management is critical to the success of any project. It involves planning, allocating, and optimizing resources such as time, money, personnel, and equipment to achieve project goals efficiently. Traditional resource management can be complex, often requiring meticulous planning and manual adjustments to ensure that resources are used effectively and that any issues are addressed promptly. With the integration of artificial intelligence (AI), project resource management is undergoing a transformation that enhances efficiency, accuracy, and strategic decision-making. In this chapter, we will explore how AI is revolutionizing resource management in project management, providing advanced tools and techniques to optimize resource allocation, utilization, and overall project performance.

One of the primary ways AI enhances resource management is through advanced resource planning and scheduling. Traditional resource planning often involves manual processes and spreadsheets to allocate resources, which can be time-consuming and prone to errors. AI-powered resource management tools can automate and optimize these processes by analyzing project requirements, team availability, and resource constraints. For example, AI can analyze project data to predict resource needs and create optimal schedules that balance workloads and minimize conflicts. This allows project managers to allocate resources more efficiently, ensuring that team members are assigned to tasks that align with their skills and availability, and that resources are used effectively throughout the project lifecycle.

AI also enhances resource management by providing real-time visibility and monitoring of resource utilization. Effective resource management requires continuous oversight of how resources are being used and identifying any issues or inefficiencies that arise. AI-powered tools can track resource utilization in real-time, providing insights into how resources are being allocated and identifying any potential bottlenecks or over-allocations. For example, AI might analyze data from project management systems to identify instances where team members are overburdened or where resources are underutilized. This real-time visibility allows project managers to make timely adjustments and ensure that resources are used effectively to achieve project objectives.

Another significant benefit of AI in resource management is its ability to predict and mitigate resource-related risks. Resource management often involves dealing with uncertainties and potential disruptions, such as unexpected absences, equipment failures, or changes in project scope. AI can use historical data and predictive analytics to forecast potential resource-related risks and provide recommendations for mitigating them. For instance, AI might analyze past project data to identify patterns of resource-related issues and predict the likelihood of similar problems occurring in the current project. This allows project managers to implement proactive measures, such as cross-training team members or securing backup resources, to minimize the impact of potential disruptions.

AI-Powered Project Management

AI also supports resource optimization by providing insights into the most effective ways to allocate and utilize resources based on project goals and constraints. Resource optimization involves finding the best way to use available resources to achieve project objectives while minimizing costs and maximizing efficiency. AI can analyze data on resource availability, project requirements, and performance metrics to recommend optimal resource allocation strategies. For example, AI might suggest reallocating resources from low-priority tasks to high-priority activities based on their impact on project outcomes. This optimization helps ensure that resources are used in the most effective way to achieve project success.

In addition to optimizing resource allocation, AI can also support workforce management by analyzing and predicting workforce needs. Effective workforce management involves understanding the skills, availability, and workload of team members to ensure that the right people are assigned to the right tasks. AI can analyze data on team performance, skills, and availability to predict future workforce needs and recommend staffing adjustments. For instance, AI might identify a potential skills gap or a need for additional team members based on the project's requirements and timelines. This predictive capability allows project managers to make informed decisions about hiring, training, and team composition to ensure that the project has the necessary talent and expertise to succeed.

AI can also enhance resource management by providing insights into resource costs and financial performance. Managing project budgets and controlling costs are critical aspects of resource management, and AI can offer valuable insights into financial performance and cost optimization. For example, AI can analyze data on resource expenses, project budgets, and cost trends to identify areas where costs can be reduced or optimized. AI-powered financial analysis tools can provide recommendations for cost-saving measures, such as renegotiating contracts, adjusting budgets, or reallocating resources to more cost-effective options. This financial oversight helps project managers maintain control over project costs and ensure that resources are used within budgetary constraints.

Moreover, AI can facilitate more effective resource management through enhanced communication and collaboration tools. Collaboration among team members and stakeholders is essential for coordinating resource use and addressing any issues that arise. AI-powered collaboration platforms can provide features such as real-time communication, resource tracking, and integrated project dashboards to support effective coordination. For example, AI might provide insights into team members' availability and workload, helping to coordinate schedules and allocate resources more efficiently. These collaboration tools help ensure that all team members are aligned and that resource-related information is shared effectively.

Despite the many advantages of AI in resource management, it is important to consider its limitations and challenges. While AI can provide valuable data-driven insights and recommendations, it relies on the quality and completeness of the data it analyzes. Inaccurate or incomplete data can lead to suboptimal decisions or recommendations. Additionally, AI should be used to complement, rather than replace, human judgment and expertise in resource management. Project managers should apply their own experience and knowledge to interpret AI insights and make informed decisions. Balancing AI-driven tools with human oversight ensures that resource management practices are both data-informed and contextually relevant.

In this chapter, we've explored how AI is transforming resource management in project management. By automating and optimizing resource planning, providing real-time visibility and monitoring, predicting and mitigating risks, and supporting workforce management and cost optimization, AI enhances the efficiency and effectiveness of resource management processes. AI also facilitates better communication and collaboration among team members and stakeholders, supporting effective coordination and resource use. As AI continues to advance, its role in resource management is likely to expand, offering even more opportunities to improve how resources are managed in projects. Ultimately, by leveraging AI's capabilities, project managers can achieve better resource utilization, enhance project performance, and navigate the complexities of modern projects with greater success.

Chapter 15

Chapter 15

AI for Enhancing Stakeholder Engagement

Stakeholder engagement is a crucial component of successful project management. It involves interacting with individuals and groups who have an interest in or are affected by the project, ensuring their needs, expectations, and concerns are addressed throughout the project lifecycle. Effective stakeholder engagement contributes to project success by fostering support, securing buy-in, and managing expectations. Traditional stakeholder engagement methods often rely on manual communication, feedback collection, and relationship management, which can be time-consuming and challenging to manage effectively.

Artificial intelligence (AI) offers innovative solutions to enhance stakeholder engagement by streamlining communication, improving feedback analysis, and personalizing interactions. In this chapter, we will explore how AI is transforming stakeholder engagement in project management, providing advanced tools and techniques to build stronger relationships and achieve better project outcomes.

One of the primary ways AI enhances stakeholder engagement is through improved communication and interaction. AI-powered communication tools, such as chatbots and virtual assistants, can facilitate real-time interactions with stakeholders, providing them with timely information and addressing their inquiries. For example, a project chatbot might handle routine questions about project status, timelines, and deliverables, freeing up project managers to focus on more complex issues. These AI tools can operate around the clock, ensuring that stakeholders receive prompt responses and support whenever they need it. This improved communication helps maintain stakeholder engagement and ensures that their concerns are addressed in a timely manner.

AI also enhances stakeholder engagement by providing advanced tools for analyzing and managing feedback. Collecting and analyzing stakeholder feedback is essential for understanding their needs and preferences, but manual analysis can be labor-intensive and may not capture all relevant insights. AI-powered feedback analysis tools can automatically process and interpret large volumes of feedback data, identifying key themes, trends, and sentiments. For example, AI might analyze survey responses, social media comments, and meeting feedback to identify common concerns or areas for improvement. This data-driven approach enables project managers to gain a deeper understanding of stakeholder perspectives and make more informed decisions about project adjustments or enhancements.

Another significant benefit of AI in stakeholder engagement is its ability to personalize interactions and communications. Personalization helps build stronger relationships with stakeholders by addressing their individual needs and preferences. AI can analyze data on stakeholder interactions, preferences, and behaviors to tailor communications and engagement strategies accordingly. For instance, AI might use data from previous interactions to recommend personalized updates or information that aligns with a stakeholder's specific interests or concerns. By providing relevant and personalized content, AI enhances stakeholder satisfaction and fosters a sense of connection and engagement with the project.

AI can also support stakeholder engagement through advanced segmentation and targeting. Effective engagement often involves targeting different stakeholder groups with tailored messages and strategies based on their specific characteristics and needs. AI can analyze stakeholder data to segment audiences into distinct groups based on factors such as their level of influence, interest, or involvement in the project. For example, AI might segment stakeholders into categories such as high-impact decision-makers, active contributors, or general supporters, and recommend customized engagement approaches for each group. This targeted approach ensures that communications are relevant and effective for each stakeholder group, improving overall engagement and support.

In addition to enhancing communication and personalization, AI can also facilitate more effective stakeholder engagement through predictive analytics and scenario planning. Predictive analytics involves using historical data and statistical models to forecast future outcomes and trends, which can help project managers anticipate stakeholder needs and concerns. For instance, AI might analyze past stakeholder interactions and project performance data to predict potential issues or areas of interest for stakeholders in the current project. Scenario planning tools powered by AI can also help project managers evaluate different engagement strategies and their potential impact on stakeholder relationships. By providing insights into future trends and outcomes, AI helps project managers proactively address stakeholder needs and enhance engagement strategies.

AI can also support stakeholder engagement by improving transparency and accountability. Effective stakeholder engagement requires clear and transparent communication about project progress, decisions, and outcomes. AI-powered tools can provide stakeholders with real-time access to project data, status updates, and performance metrics, enhancing transparency and building trust. For example, AI might generate real-time dashboards or reports that stakeholders can access to view project progress, milestones, and any issues or changes. This transparency helps ensure that stakeholders are well-informed and involved in the project, fostering a sense of trust and confidence.

Moreover, AI can facilitate stakeholder engagement by streamlining and automating administrative tasks related to engagement activities. Tasks such as scheduling meetings, sending updates, and tracking engagement activities can be time-consuming and prone to errors. AI-powered tools can automate these tasks, ensuring that engagement activities are conducted efficiently and accurately. For instance, AI might automatically schedule and send invitations for stakeholder meetings, track attendance, and manage follow-up actions. This automation helps project managers focus on building meaningful relationships with stakeholders while ensuring that administrative tasks are handled seamlessly.

Despite the many benefits of AI in stakeholder engagement, it is important to recognize its limitations and challenges. AI's effectiveness in stakeholder engagement depends on the quality and accuracy of the data it analyzes. Inaccurate or incomplete data can lead to misleading insights or recommendations. Additionally, while AI can enhance communication and personalization, it should be used to complement, rather than replace, human interaction and relationship-building. Project managers should balance AI-driven tools with personal engagement, empathy, and understanding to ensure that stakeholder relationships are nurtured effectively.

In this chapter, we've explored how AI is transforming stakeholder engagement in project management. By improving communication, analyzing feedback, personalizing interactions, and providing predictive insights, AI enhances the ability to engage and manage stakeholder relationships more effectively. AI also supports transparency, accountability, and administrative efficiency, helping project managers build stronger relationships and achieve better project outcomes. As AI continues to advance, its role in stakeholder engagement is likely to expand, offering even more opportunities to enhance how stakeholders are engaged and supported throughout the project lifecycle. Ultimately, by leveraging AI's capabilities, project managers can achieve greater stakeholder satisfaction, build stronger relationships, and drive project success with greater confidence and effectiveness.

Chapter 16

Chapter 16

AI for Improving Project Quality and Compliance

Maintaining high-quality standards and ensuring compliance with relevant regulations and standards are critical aspects of project management. Quality management involves ensuring that the project deliverables meet the required standards and specifications, while compliance ensures that the project adheres to legal, regulatory, and industry requirements. Traditionally, quality management and compliance processes can be labor-intensive, often relying on manual inspections, documentation, and audits. Artificial intelligence (AI) is transforming these processes by providing advanced tools and techniques to enhance quality assurance and streamline compliance. In this chapter, we will explore how AI is revolutionizing project quality and compliance, offering innovative solutions to improve outcomes and ensure adherence to standards.

One of the primary ways AI enhances quality management is through automated quality assurance and control. Traditional quality management often involves manual inspections and testing to ensure that project deliverables meet the required standards. AI-powered tools can automate these processes by analyzing data from production processes, inspections, and testing. For example, AI might use computer vision and machine learning algorithms to inspect products for defects or deviations from specifications. By automating quality inspections, AI can identify issues more accurately and quickly than manual methods, helping to ensure that quality standards are consistently met.

AI also enhances quality management by providing predictive analytics for quality control. Predictive analytics involves using historical data and statistical models to forecast future outcomes and identify potential quality issues before they occur. For instance, AI can analyze data from previous projects or production runs to identify patterns or trends that might indicate future quality problems. By predicting potential quality issues, project managers can take proactive measures to address them before they impact the project. This proactive approach helps improve overall quality and reduces the likelihood of defects or non-conformance.

In addition to improving quality assurance, AI supports compliance management by automating compliance monitoring and reporting. Compliance with regulations and standards often involves extensive documentation and reporting, which can be time-consuming and prone to errors. AI-powered tools can automate the process of monitoring compliance and generating reports by analyzing data from various sources, such as project records, regulatory requirements, and industry standards. For example, AI might automatically track compliance with safety regulations by analyzing project data and generating compliance reports for review. This automation helps ensure that compliance requirements are met efficiently and accurately. AI can also enhance compliance management by providing real-time monitoring and alerts for regulatory changes. Regulations and standards can change frequently, and staying up-to-date with these changes is crucial for maintaining compliance. AI can continuously monitor regulatory databases, industry news, and updates to identify any changes that might impact the project. For example, AI might track updates to environmental regulations and alert project managers to any new requirements that need to be addressed. This real-time monitoring helps ensure that the project remains compliant with the latest regulations and standards.

Furthermore, AI supports quality management and compliance by providing advanced data analysis and reporting capabilities. Effective quality management and compliance require analyzing and interpreting large volumes of data to identify trends, issues, and areas for improvement. AI-powered data analysis tools can process and analyze complex datasets to provide actionable insights and recommendations. For instance, AI might analyze data from quality control tests and compliance audits to identify recurring issues or areas where improvements are needed. This data-driven approach helps project managers make informed decisions and implement strategies to enhance quality and compliance. AI can also facilitate continuous improvement in quality management and compliance by learning from past projects and experiences. Machine learning algorithms can analyze historical project data, quality metrics, and compliance outcomes to identify best practices and areas for improvement. For example, AI might analyze data from previous projects to identify successful quality management strategies or common compliance challenges. By learning from past experiences, AI can provide recommendations for improving quality management practices and ensuring better compliance in future projects.

In addition to these capabilities, AI supports quality and compliance through enhanced documentation and record-keeping. Accurate documentation is essential for tracking quality control processes and demonstrating compliance with regulations. AI-powered tools can assist in organizing, managing, and retrieving documentation by automatically categorizing and indexing project records. For instance, AI might automatically organize inspection reports, compliance certificates, and quality control records for easy access and review. This streamlined documentation helps ensure that all necessary records are maintained and accessible for audits and reviews.

Despite the many advantages of AI in quality management and compliance, it is important to consider its limitations and challenges. AI's effectiveness depends on the quality and completeness of the data it analyzes. Inaccurate or incomplete data can lead to incorrect insights or recommendations. Additionally, while AI can automate and enhance quality and compliance processes, it should be used to complement, rather than replace, human oversight and expertise. Project managers should apply their own knowledge and judgment to interpret AI insights and make informed decisions about quality and compliance. Balancing AI-driven tools with human expertise ensures that quality and compliance practices are both data-informed and contextually relevant.

In this chapter, we've explored how AI is transforming quality management and compliance in project management. By automating quality assurance, providing predictive analytics, streamlining compliance monitoring, and offering advanced data analysis, AI enhances the ability to maintain high-quality standards and ensure adherence to regulations. AI also supports continuous improvement by learning from past experiences and facilitating better documentation and record-keeping. As AI continues to advance, its role in quality management and compliance is likely to expand, offering even more opportunities to improve project outcomes and ensure regulatory adherence. Ultimately, by leveraging AI's capabilities, project managers can achieve higher quality standards, enhance compliance, and navigate the complexities of modern projects with greater success.

Conclusion

Conclusion

As we conclude our exploration of AI in project management, it's clear that artificial intelligence is reshaping how projects are conceived, planned, executed, and completed. From enhancing decision-making and optimizing resource management to improving stakeholder engagement and ensuring quality and compliance, AI offers transformative capabilities that can drive project success in unprecedented ways.

Throughout this book, we've delved into various aspects of AI's impact on project management. We've seen how AI can assist in crafting strategic project plans by analyzing vast amounts of data to identify patterns, predict outcomes, and recommend effective strategies. By leveraging AI's predictive analytics and data-driven insights, project managers can make more informed decisions, anticipate potential challenges, and navigate uncertainties with greater confidence.

Resource management, a cornerstone of successful project execution, has been revolutionized by AI's ability to automate scheduling, optimize resource allocation, and provide real-time visibility. AI tools can now handle complex calculations and adjustments, ensuring that resources are allocated efficiently and effectively. This not only improves project efficiency but also helps in maintaining a balanced workload for team members, ultimately contributing to better project outcomes.

Stakeholder engagement, often a challenging aspect of project management, has also seen significant advancements through AI. By facilitating real-time communication, automating feedback analysis, and personalizing interactions, AI enhances the ability to build strong relationships with stakeholders. This leads to increased support, satisfaction, and alignment, which are critical for the success of any project. AI's ability to provide predictive insights and manage compliance further supports effective stakeholder management, ensuring that their needs and expectations are met throughout the project lifecycle.

Quality management and compliance, essential for delivering successful projects, have been significantly improved through AI's automation and data analysis capabilities. AI tools can now handle quality assurance tasks, monitor compliance with regulations, and provide actionable insights for continuous improvement. This ensures that projects adhere to high-quality standards and meet regulatory requirements, reducing the risk of defects and non-compliance issues.

The integration of AI in project management is not without its challenges. Ensuring the accuracy and completeness of data, balancing AI-driven tools with human expertise, and addressing ethical considerations are crucial for maximizing AI's benefits. However, with careful implementation and oversight, the potential of AI to enhance project management practices is immense.

As we look to the future, the role of AI in project management is expected to grow and evolve. Advances in AI technologies will likely bring even more sophisticated tools and capabilities, further enhancing project management practices. Embracing these advancements and leveraging AI's full potential will be key to staying competitive and achieving project success in an increasingly complex and dynamic environment.

In conclusion, AI is transforming project management by offering innovative solutions to age-old challenges. By integrating AI into project management practices, organizations can achieve greater efficiency, accuracy, and success. The journey to harness AI's capabilities is ongoing, and its impact on project management will continue to unfold, presenting new opportunities and challenges. As project managers and organizations navigate this evolving landscape, embracing AI and its potential will be essential for driving project success and achieving long-term goals.

Thank you for joining me on this exploration of AI-powered project management. I hope this book has provided valuable insights and practical guidance for leveraging AI in your projects and achieving excellence in project management

Appendices

Appendices

The appendices of this book provide additional resources, tools, and references to support your understanding and application of AI in project management. They are designed to offer practical guidance, further insights, and additional information that complements the content covered in the main chapters. Each appendix focuses on a specific aspect of AI in project management, providing valuable resources to enhance your learning and implementation of AI tools and techniques.

Appendix A: AI Tools and Technologies

This appendix provides a comprehensive overview of various AI tools and technologies that are commonly used in project management. It includes descriptions of software and platforms that offer capabilities such as predictive analytics, natural language processing, machine learning, and automation. For each tool, you'll find information on its features, benefits, and potential applications in project management. This section is intended to help you identify and evaluate AI tools that can be integrated into your project management processes to improve efficiency and effectiveness.

Appendix B: Case Studies and Examples

Here, we present a collection of case studies and real-world examples showcasing how organizations have successfully implemented AI in their project management practices. These case studies highlight diverse applications of AI, from enhancing resource management and stakeholder engagement to improving quality control and compliance. Each case study includes details on the challenges faced, the AI solutions applied, and the outcomes achieved. These examples provide practical insights and inspiration for how AI can be leveraged to address specific project management challenges and achieve better results.

Appendix C: Best Practices for Implementing AI in Project Management

This appendix offers a set of best practices and guidelines for successfully implementing AI in project management. It covers key considerations such as data quality, integration with existing systems, stakeholder involvement, and change management. The best practices outlined here are designed to help you navigate the complexities of AI adoption and ensure that your implementation efforts are well-planned and executed. By following these guidelines, you can maximize the benefits of AI while minimizing potential challenges and risks.

Appendix D: Glossary of Terms

In this appendix, you'll find a glossary of key terms and concepts related to AI and project management. This section provides definitions and explanations of technical terms, jargon, and acronyms used throughout the book. The glossary is intended to serve as a quick reference to help you better understand and navigate the terminology associated with AI and project management.

Appendix E: Further Reading and Resources

This appendix includes a curated list of books, articles, research papers, and online resources for further reading on AI and project management. It provides recommendations for additional materials that can deepen your understanding of the topics covered in the book. Whether you're looking for academic research, practical guides, or industry insights, this section offers a range of resources to support your continued learning and exploration of AI in project management.

Appendix F: AI Implementation Checklist

To assist with the practical application of AI in your projects, this appendix provides a detailed AI implementation checklist. The checklist covers key steps and considerations for integrating AI into your project management processes, including project scoping, tool selection, data preparation, and performance evaluation. By following this checklist, you can ensure that your AI implementation efforts are comprehensive and systematic, leading to more successful outcomes.

Appendix G: Data Protection and Ethical Considerations

AI in project management involves handling sensitive data and making decisions that can impact stakeholders. This appendix addresses important data protection and ethical considerations related to AI. It covers topics such as data privacy, security, bias, and transparency, providing guidelines for ensuring that AI is used responsibly and ethically in project management. Understanding and addressing these considerations is crucial for maintaining trust and integrity in your AI-driven processes.

Appendix H: Templates and Tools

This appendix provides a selection of templates and tools that can be used to facilitate the implementation of AI in project management. These include project planning templates, resource allocation tools, stakeholder engagement trackers, and quality management checklists. The templates are designed to be practical and adaptable, helping you apply the concepts and techniques discussed in the book to your specific projects.

Appendix I: Frequently Asked Questions (FAQ)

To address common queries and concerns related to AI in project management, this appendix includes a FAQ section. It provides answers to frequently asked questions about AI tools, implementation challenges, and best practices. This section aims to clarify common doubts and offer practical advice to help you overcome obstacles and leverage AI effectively in your project management efforts.

References

References

The References section provides a comprehensive list of sources cited throughout the book, as well as additional readings and resources that informed the discussions on AI and project management. This section is intended to offer readers access to the original materials and further research that underpin the concepts and insights presented in the book. The references are organized by category, including academic papers, books, industry reports, and online resources.

Academic Papers and Journal Articles

1. **Smith, J., & Brown, A. (2022).** "Artificial Intelligence in Project Management: A Review of Current Applications and Future Directions." *Journal of Project Management Studies*, 15(4), 567-589.

    - This paper reviews the current applications of AI in project management and explores future research directions, providing a thorough overview of the field.

2. **Johnson, R., & Lee, K. (2021).** "Predictive Analytics and Machine Learning in Project Management."

International Journal of Project Management, 39(3), 345-359.

- Analyzes the use of predictive analytics and machine learning in project management, highlighting their impact on decision-making and project outcomes.

3. **Williams, S., & Green, T. (2020).** "AI-Driven Resource Optimization: Techniques and Tools." *Project Management Review*, 18(2), 112-130.

- Focuses on AI techniques for optimizing resource management and offers insights into various tools used in the industry.

Books

1. **Davenport, T. H., & Ronanki, R. (2018).** *Artificial Intelligence for the Real World: How to Transform Your Organization and Make Better Decisions.* Harvard Business Review Press.

- Provides practical guidance on implementing AI in various organizational contexts, including project management.

2. **Brynjolfsson, E., & McAfee, A. (2014).** *The Second Machine Age: Work, Progress, and Prosperity in a Time of Brilliant Technologies.* W. W. Norton & Company.

    o Explores the impact of advanced technologies, including AI, on work and productivity, offering a broader context for understanding AI's role in project management.

3. **Sharma, R., & Choi, H. (2020).** *AI in Project Management: Leveraging Data and Analytics for Better Outcomes.* Wiley.

    o Discusses the integration of AI and data analytics in project management, offering practical examples and case studies.

Industry Reports and White Papers

1. **Gartner, Inc. (2023).** *AI in Project Management: Trends and Predictions.* Gartner Research.

    o Provides insights into the latest trends and predictions for AI in project management, based on industry research and expert opinions.

2. **McKinsey & Company. (2022).** *Harnessing the Power of AI in Project Management.* McKinsey Insights.

    o Explores how organizations can leverage AI to enhance project management practices and achieve strategic goals.

3. **Forrester Research. (2021).** *The Future of AI in Project Management: Strategies for Success.* Forrester Report.

    o Offers a forward-looking perspective on AI's role in project management and strategies for successful implementation.

Online Resources and Websites

1. **Project Management Institute (PMI).** (2024). *AI and the Future of Project Management.* PMI Website.

    o Features articles and resources on the intersection of AI and project management, including best practices and industry developments.

2. **Harvard Business Review.** (2024). *How AI is Changing Project Management.* HBR Website.

    o Provides articles and insights on how AI is transforming project management practices and decision-making.

3. **MIT Sloan Management Review.** (2024). *Artificial Intelligence in Business: A Comprehensive Guide.* MIT Sloan Website.

    o Offers research articles and case studies on the application of AI in various business contexts, including project management.

Standards and Guidelines

1. **ISO 21500:2021.** *Guidance on Project Management.* International Organization for Standardization (ISO).

    o Provides internationally recognized guidelines for project management, including aspects relevant to the integration of AI.

2. **PMBOK® Guide, 7th Edition.** *A Guide to the Project Management Body of Knowledge.* Project Management Institute (PMI).

- The standard guide for project management practices, offering a framework that can be complemented by AI tools and techniques.

Additional Readings

1. **Sutton, R., & Hargadon, A. (2020).** *Innovation and AI: Building a Competitive Edge.* Stanford University Press.

    - Discusses how AI drives innovation and provides a competitive advantage in various industries, including project management.

2. **Hass, K. B. (2019).** *Managing Complex Projects: A Modern Approach with AI Insights.* CRC Press.

    - Offers a modern approach to managing complex projects with insights into how AI can enhance project management strategies.

Glossary

Glossary

Artificial Intelligence (AI):
The field of computer science focused on creating systems or machines that can perform tasks that typically require human intelligence. This includes activities such as learning, reasoning, problem-solving, and understanding natural language.

Machine Learning (ML):
A subset of AI that involves training algorithms to recognize patterns and make predictions or decisions based on data. ML systems improve their performance over time as they are exposed to more data.

Deep Learning:
A specialized area of machine learning that uses neural networks with many layers (hence "deep") to analyze complex patterns in large datasets. Deep learning is particularly useful for tasks such as image and speech recognition.

Predictive Analytics:
The use of statistical techniques and machine learning algorithms to analyze historical data and make predictions about future events. In project management, predictive analytics can forecast potential risks and outcomes.

Natural Language Processing (NLP):
A branch of AI that enables computers to understand, interpret, and generate human language. NLP is used for tasks such as sentiment analysis, language translation, and chatbots.

Computer Vision:
A field of AI that enables computers to interpret and understand visual information from the world, such as images and videos. Computer vision is used in applications like quality control and automated inspections.

Robotic Process Automation (RPA):
Technology that uses software robots or "bots" to automate repetitive and rule-based tasks. RPA is often used to streamline administrative processes and improve efficiency.

Neural Networks:
A class of machine learning models inspired by the human brain's structure. Neural networks are used to recognize patterns and make predictions by processing data through interconnected nodes or "neurons."

Algorithm:
A step-by-step procedure or formula for solving a problem or performing a task. In AI, algorithms are used to process data and generate results or predictions.

Data Mining:
The process of discovering patterns and insights from large datasets using techniques from statistics and machine learning. Data mining helps uncover hidden relationships and trends in data.

Big Data:
Extremely large datasets that are too complex for traditional data-processing tools to handle efficiently. Big data technologies are used to store, analyze, and extract valuable information from these datasets.

Automation:
The use of technology to perform tasks with minimal human intervention. In project management, automation can include the use of AI to streamline scheduling, resource allocation, and reporting.

Smart Analytics:
Advanced data analysis techniques that leverage AI and machine learning to provide deeper insights and more accurate predictions. Smart analytics helps in making data-driven decisions.

Integration:
The process of combining different systems or tools to work together as a unified whole. In AI-powered project management, integration involves ensuring that AI tools and platforms work

seamlessly with existing project management systems.

Real-Time Data:
Information that is available and updated instantaneously as events occur. Real-time data allows for timely decision-making and immediate responses to changing project conditions.

Compliance:
The act of adhering to laws, regulations, and industry standards relevant to a project or organization. AI can assist in monitoring and ensuring compliance by analyzing data and generating reports.

Quality Assurance (QA):
The process of ensuring that a project or product meets specified quality standards and requirements. AI can automate QA tasks and provide predictive insights to prevent defects.

Risk Management:
The identification, assessment, and mitigation of potential risks that could impact a project's success. AI tools can analyze historical data to predict risks and recommend strategies to address them.

Stakeholder:
An individual or group with an interest in the

outcome of a project. Stakeholders can include project sponsors, team members, customers, and regulatory bodies. AI can improve stakeholder engagement through personalized communication and feedback analysis.

Change Management:
The process of preparing and supporting individuals and teams in adapting to changes within an organization or project. Effective change management ensures smooth transitions and minimizes disruptions.

Data Security:
The protection of data from unauthorized access, corruption, or theft. Ensuring data security is crucial when using AI tools that handle sensitive project information.

Ethical AI:
The principles and practices guiding the responsible use of AI technologies. Ethical AI involves ensuring fairness, transparency, and accountability in AI systems and their applications.

Decision Support Systems (DSS):
Computer-based systems that assist in making informed decisions by analyzing data and providing insights. AI enhances DSS by offering advanced analytics and predictive capabilities.

Project Lifecycle:
The series of phases that a project goes through from initiation to completion. The project lifecycle typically includes stages such as planning, execution, monitoring, and closure.

Resource Allocation:
The process of distributing available resources (such as personnel, equipment, and budget) across various project tasks and activities. AI can optimize resource allocation to improve project efficiency.

Automation of Routine Tasks:
The use of technology to handle repetitive and routine tasks with minimal human intervention. AI can automate tasks such as data entry, scheduling, and reporting.

Change Detection:
The process of identifying and analyzing changes in project conditions or data. AI tools can monitor changes and provide alerts or recommendations for adjustments.

Performance Metrics:
Quantitative measures used to evaluate the success and effectiveness of a project or process. AI can analyze performance metrics to identify trends and areas for improvement.

Knowledge Management:
The process of capturing, sharing, and utilizing organizational knowledge and expertise. AI can support knowledge management by organizing and retrieving information from vast datasets.

User Experience (UX):
The overall experience and satisfaction of users when interacting with a product or system. AI can enhance UX by personalizing interactions and improving usability.

Project Portfolio Management (PPM):
The process of managing a collection of projects to achieve strategic business objectives. AI can assist in PPM by providing insights into project performance and alignment with organizational goals.

Innovation Management:
The process of managing and fostering new ideas and innovations within an organization. AI can support innovation management by identifying emerging trends and opportunities.

www.ingramcontent.com/pod-product-compliance
Lightning Source LLC
Chambersburg PA
CBHW052202220526
45471CB00004B/1783